Second edition; first printing in 2023

Copyright © 2022 Martina & Hans Thörn Durefelt Helförlag

ISBN 978-91-86889-15-9

www.hansmartinatwinflames.com

Contents

Part 1 - Healing & Energy Work

Part 2 - Blockages & Healing

Let your longing lead you home,
home to your soul & your heart.

.

INTRODUCTION

We, Martina and Hans, are Twin Flames. We work as spiritual teachers, authors, guides, and intuitive healers. Through the last years, we have worked thousands of hours with our inner self and with clients in different ways. We want to share the knowledge we have gathered over the years, and we hope that this book can contribute with support, development, and inspiration on your spiritual journey.

In this book, you will have the opportunity to delve into your inner self in many different ways. The text in the book acts as a guide and leads you into your innermost core, your soul. We can look for the answers on the outside, but it is only when we turn our eyes inward that our real journey begins. When we really begin to face what is within us - all that we have turned away from for so long - that is when deep healing begins to take place and we are transformed.

If you are reading this text, you are most likely an old soul who has walked many lives here on earth. Old souls often feel misunderstood and alone here on earth, like they don't fit in anywhere. If this applies to you, we want to give you some hope along the way. You are not alone, and it will get better! An important key here is to let go of everything that we carry and that is not ours to carry. Everything we caught inside, which was never meant for us. Most people we come into contact with live their lives based on other people's expectations. They are busy trying to fulfill their parents' dreams or to fit into society's norms. But to truly find true joy and freedom, you need to find your own truth and what enriches you and your soul. You need to peel away everything that shaped and limited you - through upbringing, past life, and surroundings - to find who you really are. For many, this is a long journey, the journey called life.

The greatest thing we can do in this life is find our way back to ourselves, find our gifts and give them away. Living through one's divine light is the very foundation or essence of Light work. You who hold this book in your hand are a light worker and when you find your inner light, you light up the world for people around you. You are healing the planet and raising its frequency more than you may realize. Imagine that every time you think a loving thought or every time you do something with love, that energy vibrates and spreads out into the Universe.

Take a moment and consider the following questions:
- Behind all the fears - who am I?
- Behind all the masks - who am I?
- Behind everyone's expectations - who am I?
- Behind my upbringing - who am I?
- Behind all the musts – who am I?
- Behind all the adaptation – who am I?

This book consists of a lot of information and exercises, all to contribute with help and understanding on your spiritual journey. Based on our own work, higher guidance, and many client sessions, we have carefully selected the blockages and limitations that are included in the book. It is our opinion that the further we get on our journey, the more we need to look at and work with. We peel back layer by layer, to finally get to the core.

Many times, it is not enough to work with a certain chakra or with one type of healing. We need to see the complexity of us humans and work with many different parts within ourselves. It can be challenging, but incredibly healing when we begin to see patterns we have or when we find deep blockages that we are given the opportunity to heal.

Don't forget that you are amazing, and you can do anything! How do we know that? Well, because you've lived hundreds of lives before and made it all the way to here! Become aware of your soul's immense power and ability to heal. It may sound cliche, but YOU have the ability to heal everything within you.

Hans' Life Story

I am an old soul, a starseed and Twin Flame. I grew up in Sweden, in an environment that made it difficult for me to be myself in a lot of ways. It wasn't that there was anything wrong with the surroundings, and my family was kind and supporting. But I was different, and I had a strong sensitivity. Through my social qualities, I could fit in anywhere on paper and I was considered popular and even successful. But I was lost, not only in myself but in how I lived my life in general. I lived my life by adapting to please others. I have lived several past lives where it was a struggle between life and death, as it often is here on Earth and in these lower frequencies. Throughout my life I have had a variety of relationships, one more challenging than the other. What they all had in common was that I gave and gave without getting much in return. After several years in a heavy negative karmic relationship, I was exhausted, not only within myself but in life in general. I longed to end the pain I was carrying.

In the middle of all this, Martina appeared and somehow, she saved me, or she helped me save myself. She not only gave me joy back in life but also encouraged me daily to dare to be myself in all situations. It was a tough fight as I neglected myself and my self-worth for many years. But now I have come so far that I can truly say that I love myself, my life and of course Martina and my three beautiful children. They give me so much just by being who they are.

Before I met Martina, I searched all my life for answers to why I felt so miserable. I went through elementary school, high school and even university where I felt increasingly worse. I also tried a normal working life as a company manager, but soon realized that it wouldn't work. I just felt worse and worse with anxiety and various forms of physical and emotional ailments. In the end it didn't work anymore, and I got burned out. I had ME, could only tolerate 5 foods, was sensitive to electricity and had difficulty being around other people due to my sensitivity. So, what would I do with my life? By coincidence (or synchronicity) I ended up on a healing course many years ago. I didn't think I had what it took to give healing but the leader who ran the course said I had everything needed to do this at a high level. What he said resonated as truth for me and from that day (25 years ago) I have worked with healing and intuitive guidance in various ways.

Today Martina and I work with clients all over the world, with topics such as twin flames, soul connections, old souls, high sensitivity, and starseeds. We focus on active intuitive healing, which we describe thoroughly in the book. Through the years, I have become my own healer. Before my work started with Martina, I developed something called the Soulbalance method, a method for self-healing and for finding blockages within oneself. It became a very popular method and at most there were about 200 trained coaches in this method.

When I met Martina, I thought I had healed most of myself with the Soulbalance Method. But that was not the case. Through the healing that was both deep and necessary, I am now here today, and I want to tell you that - nothing is impossible - if we don't believe it ourselves.

Martina and I hope with this book to give you the tools you need to be able to heal yourself on a deep soul level and from that, become your own healer. You were born free and now we want to help you free yourself from past wounds.

Martina's Life Story

I was born into a family consisting of my parents and my two sisters. As a child I was very sensitive and due to some things, that happened I was forced to shut down this sensitivity early on. It is only many years later that I gradually understood that I am an old soul, highly sensitive and a starseed - with the life task of healing myself and helping other people on their journey.

I have always been a thinker and my thoughts have been both my burden and my gift. With the help of my thoughts, I have learned to understand things in depth and that led me into studies about humans' behavior, therapy, psychology, and spirituality. The hard part has consisted of destructive thoughts about myself, fears, obsessions, and this started when I was around 11 years old. At that age I was very anxious, and I struggled with a lot of inner pain and fear attached to my thoughts. I did not understand then that many of these heavy layers inside of me were traumas from previous lifetimes. Above all, there is a past life that recurred a lot in this life and that I had to do a lot of work on. In that life I was a Shaman and native American in North America. I lived together with Hans, and we were a couple. In that life I lost my family, my spirituality and myself when I was captured and then murdered. This has left a deep mark on me and that life, along with other lives made me shut down my spiritual side and lose faith in myself. I wrestled with an extreme amount of darkness even as a child, darkness that found its way in as fears. This was tough for me because. I believe in the light and that faith has helped me many times in life.

My childhood had its glimmers of light but also its hard parts. I grew up in an existence that was affected by a trauma that happened back in time. In addition to that, I struggled a lot with myself, especially in my teenage years where I felt different and strange. In high school, I fell into a black whole, because I felt that everything was pointless. But then something happened that changed my life forever.

I read a book called "Enveloped by Light", a book about a near-death experience. This book resonated deeply with my soul essence (without me realizing it at the time) and opened my eyes to spirituality. This gave me new hope for life and as soon as I turned 18, I made an appointment with my first medium. Early on, spirituality became my great driving force and passion in life. It gave me comfort and I knew there was a meaning to everything I had experienced.

When I was 23 years old, I entered into a relationship that would become a deep and heavy struggle for myself for 10 years. It was a karmic relationship, with great connections back in past lives. In connection with this meeting, a lot of traumatic feelings, darkness, heaviness, and pain from past lives came up. This was totally overwhelming for me and to cope with it all I started taking anti-depressants. I shut down everything - my feelings, thoughts, intuition, and everything that was really pushing to come up and heal. I shut down my life and went into a darkness that lasted for many years. It was as if the happy and hopeful part of me was gone.

It was only several years later, when Hans came into the picture, that my life changed and started to go in the right direction. Hans helped me out of the situation I was in and together we have built a business where we help others heal, get out of difficult situations and relationships. There is as much to write about this as possible, but I will content myself with saying this – Hans helped me in every way you can help another person. He took me from the place that had become a prison to the place where I was supposed to be.

It is my and our great desire to guide you home to your soul and your heart.

PART 1

HEALING & ENERGY WORK

Chapter 1

ENERGY, HEALING AND
OUR SOUL ORIGIN

Whatever you carry can be healed! It is our conviction, after having seen major processes happen – both in ourselves and in other people. However, it may require patience, courage, and determination. Healing our inner self can be the most challenging thing we go through, because we need to face ourselves at all levels. We need to be willing to pick up what is hidden, look at what limits us, and then let it go. We have noticed that old souls, as a rule, always carry large and complex things, both from this life and from previous lives. It can be trauma or events that are in our past but that affect our everyday life here and now. In order to heal and step into our full potential, we need to understand ourselves and who we are.

Our Soul Energy & our Origin

We are souls who have chosen to incarnate here on earth in a physical body for the purpose of learning, release old stuff, expanding and raising our vibration. We live in a Universe where everything vibrates at different levels and frequencies. It is precisely what causes different dimensions to be created and it is also what causes us to perceive our surroundings here on earth as physical. The higher up in dimensions we go the thinner the energy becomes and the lower we go the more compact it becomes. Matter is just energy particles brought together and vibrating at a similar level, a compact and heavy vibration. Everything we see around us in life and everyone we meet sends out vibrations, vibrations that we take in and manage in our energy system.

If we are energy sensitive, we will pick up a lot of this energy around us and even take it in as our own.

In order for our physical body to be alive, function optimally and be able to provide us with what we need during life, we constantly get access to life energy from the Divine Source, our origin. This life energy flows into our body and is captured by the energy centers located in our energy body. We have a variety of energy centers within and around us but the most common are our 7 main chakras.

Our soul vibrates at a significantly higher level than the frequency we experience here on earth. We choose to name the higher level as 5d. This is of course a simplified way of talking about it all, but it shows that we exist simultaneously on several different levels. Our soul being at a higher frequency level can see things and know what is best for us from a higher perspective, while in our physical body many times we experience and see things through our emotions and through different filters. Our ego and our fears limit our way of looking at things from a more objective way.

The more we heal and process and let go of what limits us, the more our vibration rises, and we vibrate at a higher frequency. We will then experience that life feels easier and we will have more access to all our life energy. We experience an energetic flow.

Our soul energy is passed on from life to life, meaning we pick up in this life where we left off in our last. We carry with us our inner wounds and traumas, purely energetically at the cellular level. These can be activated under various circumstances in this life, for example when we meet a certain person, encounter something or experience a strong emotional event.

What is Healing?

According to us, healing is all the inner work we do within ourselves to become more balanced, more whole as beings, and more in touch with our soul – our true self. Examples of how you can work with healing are through energy work, clearing blockages, balancing the chakras, and healing the inner child. Basically, we are energy beings and blockages are created when energy becomes locked within us in various ways. Working with healing means that we set energy that has been locked in motion, it begins to flow freely, and we experience more and more lightness and balance. We believe that all people have the ability to heal themselves, but sometimes we may need outside help to see and access things.

What is a Block and how is it created?

A blockage means that the energy is out of balance or blocked somewhere in your energy system and this is holding you back or limiting you in some way. This means that somewhere in your energy system there is an imbalance. The reason why the energy is out of balance can be due to many different factors.

Examples of how blocks can be created:

- Experience of trauma – when we experience trauma, our body reacts with very strong emotions (or thoughts). If we cannot or do not have the opportunity to handle and process these feelings, we may suppress them. We suppress the energy that comes as it becomes so powerful and overwhelming. These repressed emotions create a blockage.

- We are shaped in a certain way of what we learned in the childhood. When we then find ourselves in situations that go against what we have learned, we believe that we are/are doing wrong, and we begin to avoid certain feelings or thoughts to do the right thing or fit in.

- We may carry fears from this or past lives, which cause us to hold back or hold back parts of ourselves. Because of that, we stop the flow of energy within us - a blockage is created.

Our Divine Energy System

We can have energy blockages in several different places in our energy system. For example, we can have blockages mentally, emotionally, in our chakras, in our aura or in our physical body. Often a specific blockage can affect different parts of our energy system. The more and the bigger blockages we have within us, the more difficulties and imbalance we will experience in our life. This is because much of our life energy is blocked.

Energy cannot be destroyed; it can only change form. This means that all the energy you have inside you is there all the time and if you don't want or can't experience it in its original form, it will express itself in a different way. That's how energy works.

Example: A feeling consists of energy! If you avoid or refuse to feel the feeling, this feeling (energy) will take another expression. You may have back pain or experience great fatigue.

Important parts of our Energy System

Our energy system is our armor, just as it is our connection to our soul. It is a complex system that helps us navigate and cope with life here on earth. Below follows a description of the Energy System's basic parts.

Our Aura

Our Aura is the etheric field that surrounds our physical body. The Aura acts as an extension of our energy body but also as a protection. When we meet a person, we often feel the energy already in our Aura. At that moment, we can choose whether we want this energy (person) into our life. So, our Aura is there to protect us, even if we are often unaware of this. When we let an energy into our aura, it then passes on to our internal energy system, that is, our chakras. We can see the Aura as a kind of filter, where we can filter out what we don't want into our life. It may sound simple, but as many of us carry trauma and fears, we bring in external energy that matches this. If you carry the trauma of abuse, you may choose to bring in similar energies from outside. That lead you to choose a partner who treats you badly or takes advantage of you in some way. Many times, we are so used to running over our energy, that we don't notice when someone crosses our limits.

The aura consists of several layers. The innermost layer is close to our physical body, while the remaining layers extend several meters out.

Our 7 Energy Centers

Our Energy Centers, or our Chakras, have a great significance for how we take in and give out Energy. When we have flow in our Chakra system, energy is supplied to our physical body but also to the respective organs. Blockages in the chakra system are common and here we need to work a lot on changing the energy that limits us.

Our Emotional Energy Body

Our emotional energy body represents our emotions and how we process our emotions in everyday life. It is common for us to have large emotional blocks from childhood, especially if we are sensitive.

Our Mental Energy Body

Our mental energy body represents our thoughts and how we process our thoughts in everyday life. If we become very limited in our upbringing or if we are formed early on by strong negative belief systems, we can get big blocks here.

Our Masculine Energy

Our Masculine Energy represents our ability to think, analyze, act and manifest. The masculine energy is made up of our right side of the body.

Our Feminine Energy

Our Feminine Energy represents our ability to feel, take in, create, and give life. The feminine energy is made up of our left side of the body.

Our galactic connection

Our Galactic Connection is our connection with our higher selves, our guides and Source. When this channel is clean, we receive messages and cleansing energy that help us in the right direction.

Our connection with the Earth

Our grounding is the part of us that connects us to the earth we walk on. To feel safe and stable, we need to be grounded in ourselves. We need to anchor our energy with the earth, so that we can create the life we long for.

Generally speaking, blockages are created when we go against our soul, when we hold ourselves back, when we make choices based on fear, or when we encounter strong emotions that we cannot adequately handle.

Common to many old souls is their energy sensitivity and the fact that they grew up in a dysfunctional environment. This particular combination often leads to major blockages in the body, due to the fact that the person has not learned to manage their emotions and has often shut down their inner self. The greater our sensitivity, the more difficult it is for us to grow up in an uncomprehending and sometimes cold environment. Then the only way out may be to shut down our own needs. This is common for people who grew up with one or two parents who themselves carry great difficulties, fears, trauma, addiction, or mental imbalance.

We want to emphasize that a dysfunctional upbringing does not always mean outwardly visible traumas but is more about the child's subjective and personal experience of what happened. Let's say we grow up with a mother who is in many ways calm, kind and wants us well. But she has a hard time showing us deep love. From the outside, it looks like a calm and nice upbringing, but for us as children it can still be experienced as a trauma or as a great loss. Highly sensitive children need extra help in managing and understanding their emotions.

We often meet people in our work who believe that their upbringing was calm and balanced. But when we do a little digging, it often turns out that there are tough memories and experiences behind it. As adults, we are often good at repressing or distorting things that happened to us, because we want to protect our parents or ourselves. It is completely natural and basically the vast majority of parents want their children well. But for our inner child, the part of us that still remembers everything, it is important and valuable to look at how it was and deal with it. The needs that we do not get satisfied as children, we will look for in later relationships throughout life.

The Ego - Our inner Resistance & Fears

Our ego is part of our human structure. The ego has helped us in many ways through life. Through uncertain conditions and through dangers, the ego has acted as a bodyguard, always there to protect us and make sure we are not in danger. Our ego is not our enemy and the goal is not to turn on the ego and tell it is wrong. The goal is to show the ego and our inner fears that everything is okay. When we do things despite being afraid or experiencing resistance, our ego will eventually calm down and understand that everything is in order.

When we have experienced difficult events or a traumatic upbringing, we have many times created a strong ego, that is, a strong defense within us that does everything to protect us. When we start working with our inner self, this inner protector will make itself heard and come to the surface. The important thing then is to become aware: "Ah, now my inner resistance comes up" or "okay, my ego doesn't want me to do this". We need to become aware of it and do things anyway. We don't have to wait for the ego to approve, but we can instead try to calm our inner self. We can calm the part within us that feels resistance and know that this is a natural part of the spiritual journey.

A part of you will always feel resistance, fear, or discomfort in the face of change - that's perfectly okay. If thoughts like "I can't", "I won't be able to do this" or "I feel so much resistance" come up, try just observing it. Become aware that it is there and sink through it. Think of it as going right through it or sinking through it. The more you face it, the less the resistance will be.

It is also important to know the following: When we begin to face great things within ourselves and when we begin to take great steps on our spiritual journey, THEN inner blockages from childhood and past lives that are not resolved will surface. It can be scary because then we think something is wrong, but actually it's the opposite - we're on the RIGHT path. Dare to challenge yourself and face the fears and obstacles that come up.

High Sensitivity - Challenges & Gifts
High sensitivity is a concept that has become increasingly talked about today and it often comes up in our client conversations. Being highly sensitive or empathic means that you carry an extrasensory sensitivity, that is, you perceive everything that happens much more

strongly than people who do not have the same sensitivity. This can mean that you feel other people's feelings if you are in the same room, but also at a distance. It is also common to sense and pick up a lot of energy going on around you.

High sensitivity is very common in old souls, and it is because we develop a greater sensitivity the more lives we live here on earth. For each life and for each step we take in our inner development, the more life energy we take into the body. Our body simply becomes more and more filled with our soul, and we expand our consciousness and our energy. This sensitivity can be expressed in many ways. The most common thing is that we feel other people's feelings extra clearly. But it can also be shown through sensitivity to light, sensitivity to loud sounds, touch, smells and through how we perceive external events. As children and highly sensitive, we are often extra receptive to what happens in our surroundings, both good and bad. If we live in a warm and loving growing up environment where we get to express ourselves, it can help us develop and confirm our sensitivity. If we are highly sensitive and experience trauma or high stress as children, it can cause us to shut ourselves down, create dissociation, develop various forms of symptoms, and find it difficult to handle life in adulthood.

Being highly sensitive is an amazing gift and many with this sensitivity are incredibly empathetic, empathetic, and intuitive. They are old souls who have a long way behind them and who therefore carry a lot of wisdom and power within them. By sensing our surroundings and other people, we gain a greater understanding of what is going on. If we learn to manage, understand, and master our sensitivity, we can go as far as we want in the field of Healing.

Working with healing is about working with energy and the more we can understand our own energy, the more we can help other people. By understanding ourselves, we also understand others and vice versa.

Before we learn to manage our sensitivity, it can often feel like a burden, perhaps even something we would like to be without. For many highly sensitive souls, life becomes overwhelming, and it is not unusual for various forms of escape in the form of drugs, food addiction or other distractions. Perhaps you have heard the words Sensitivity is either a gift or a curse. There is a lot in that exact sentence. In order to be able to use our sensitivity in a positive and developing way, we need to get to know our own energy and thus be able to distinguish when other people's energies and emotions enter our energy system. Otherwise, it gets messy, and we don't know either way out or in. This may take some work but it's well worth it in the end.

Transforming Energy – A powerful Tool

When we can master energy in different forms, we become masters of our own life. In order to achieve balance and inner healing, we need to become experts on ourselves and thus manage all the energy that flows through our energy field. For old souls, turning darkness into light is a big part of the journey here on earth. It may seem tough, but that's because we're ready for it. We never get bigger experiences than our soul thinks we can handle. When we are down in periods of darkness and doubt, it is easy to give up and feel lost. Then be aware that you need to be in the dark sometimes, to learn to deal with it and transform the darkness into light.

Imagine a person with a former addiction, who lived in loneliness, heaviness, pain and who was down. Imagine that this person after a long time chooses to leave his addiction, rises from the darkness, and creates a new existence. It's not hard to imagine what a huge inner journey this person has had to make to get all the way to the other side. It is a journey of pure transformation. That's exactly how it works within ourselves.

Fear and love are two energies that vibrate at different frequencies. You can always get from one state to another with the help of your intention, will and a little work along the way. Transforming energy does not always have to be difficult, but the important thing is that we learn to get an outlet for our energy, our emotions and that we create an awareness.

Tips on how you can transform energy within you:
- Transform inner anger and frustration by hitting a pillow or screaming your anger in the car when you're alone.
- Transform stress within you by spending some time in nature.
- Work on becoming aware of how your own energy feels and clear when you feel the energy changing.
- Transform inner pain by crying and feeling all your emotions.
- Transform heavy energy from the environment by imagining how this energy dissolves and turns into a ball of light.
- Ask your higher self for help in releasing old heavy energy that no longer resonates with you and your truth.

Our inner Vibration & our outer Manifestation

The universe consists of several major conceptions, which are also called Universal Laws. These laws permeate everything around us, regardless of whether we are on Earth or in any other place. You've probably heard of the Law of Attraction - Like attracts like. This law is very important to understand if we are to work with our inner self, heal and change our existence. As we mentioned earlier, everything in the Universe consists of energy that vibrates at different frequencies. According to the Law of Attraction, this means that energy particles that are at the same frequency attract other that are at the same frequency. Translated into our body and our existence, our inner vibration controls much of what we attract into our life.

We all have a Universal Energy within us, which is a composite of everything we carry - feelings, thoughts, memories, events, etc. The more weight and unprocessed things we carry, the lower our Universal energy becomes. We can feel this ourselves in life. When we feel bad, we feel weighed down and everything becomes difficult. We easily end up in a negative spiral and the further down the spiral we get, the harder it can be to get back up. If we carry unprocessed trauma, feelings of guilt or other heavy things, this will affect our entire energy. We unconsciously attract more of the same energy into our lives. It could be people who treat us badly or other negative events.

If we turn it around, we can see the opposite. When we feel good, we get a flow in life, and everything goes more easily. Things happen at just the right moment, and we feel that everything flows. The more we heal and release what limits us, the more we raise our Universal energy. We raise our inner vibration and our outer existence changes.

When it comes to our inner vibration and what we carry, it is important that we do not judge ourselves. We all carry heavy feelings and experiences from our past, as it is part of being human. So never judge yourself in the process but see it as a goal to free yourself from old junk that drains your energy.

We are all a product of the society and environment we were born into. We carry with us memories, feelings, and events in our cells - things that we got from our parents and even further back. Already in childhood we are molded into a society where we learn how to be, act and handle things. The more we peel it away the closer we get to our own energy.

Dark Night of the Soul

Perhaps you have heard of the Dark Night of the Soul. The name has its basis in the darkness many of us encounter when we enter into a spiritual awakening. It is a period of deep purification and cleansing, where we are more or less forced to let go of things that were previously part of us. This period can be very painful and last longer or shorter for different people. Some experience this darkness for a few weeks, others for years. The purpose is to help you with liberation, so that you can let go of what is holding you back and move further and higher in your spiritual ascent.

Some experience deep pain, hopelessness, depression, or a general state of crisis. It is also common to lose sight of who you are and feel lost in your existence and among people.

The dark night of the soul can recur in installments, that is, we experience this several times during our ascension process.

Old souls often carry many things from past lives, which means there is a lot to heal in this life.

It is common to lose contact with friends and people with whom we previously had a lot in common. Sometimes it happens because we choose to leave them ourselves, but sometimes because they simply cannot be in our existence anymore. It can be painful to develop spiritually because it can lead to us needing to let go of people, situations and other things that were close to us. But carry the following words with you; Everything that is real, it always remains. Nothing that is real can disappear.

You may lose contact with people for a while but sooner or later you meet them again, in this life or in the next.

Advice for those who experience a lot of darkness:
- Be aware that it is your soul that organized this and that it is happening for your sake.
- Remember that energy is always changing, and this means that all states change. Nothing is static.
- Try to look carefully at the feelings you encounter within yourself - they show you what you need to let go of and where there are unhealed wounds within you.
- Try to get outside at least once a day or do something that gives you energy.
- Give yourself a lot of love - the reason you are here is because you are a strong old soul and because you have a lot to help others with.
- Get to know your body and energy and what it wants to convey to you.

- Trust that your guides are with you, even if it doesn't feel like it. When we are down in heaviness and darkness, it can feel as if we lose touch with the light and our guides. They are with you all the time, but it can be difficult for you to perceive it when you are down in the dark.

Chapter 2

ARE YOU A STARSEED?

Starseeds are souls that originate or have a strong energetic connection to one or more galactic locations other than Earth itself. It can mean that you have lived most of your lives in another place or that there is another strong connection to that particular place. It is thus a large part of how we as souls have been formed and depending on which place we are connected to; we will carry with us different energy gifts and qualities. In the same way that we are influenced and shaped by the environment we grow up in here on earth, we are also influenced by the previous place or places we lived a lot on.

Common characteristics & challenges for Starseeds

Most of the people we meet in our work are Starseeds. There is an endless amount to write about Starseeds, but we have selected what comes up again and again in our encounters with Starseeds.

Starseeds often feel different and a little out of place here on Earth, like they don't really belong here. There is a strong longing for home or a longing for something bigger. Starseeds often carry a great sensitivity and can feel that they have a life task, or a Soul Mission here on earth.

Many Starseeds are born into dysfunctional environments, to help transform the energy in the family and to gain the conditions needed in this life as lightworkers. The challenge for many here is that they get stuck in the burden they brought with them from growing up and are not quite able to get out of it. In order to step into our full potential and our life's mission, we first need to free ourselves from what limits us from childhood and to some extent past lives, in order to step into our light and our true power.

Starseeds are often drawn to the stars and often have a longing away, away from daily life here on earth. In principle, all the Starseeds we come into contact with have a hard time with routines and living in a classic 8-16 existence. These are souls who have a great need for freedom and to do their thing in their own way. They are what you call Free spirits and they only come into their own power when they follow their inner compass.

Something else that characterizes starseeds in particular is that they have strong healing abilities, developed intuition and a high basic energy. The high basic energy means that they have a high light and that they have a lot of energy within them. Based on that, it is extremely important that Starseeds are not restricted too much during childhood. When their high energy and power is limited, the child will turn the energy inward and at worst create emotional or physical pain later in life.

An example:
Souls from the Pleiades are often characterized by having a lot of energy, power and they have a lot of fire within them. They are creative and enjoy change, communication and can be a little impatient. Now imagine that a person from the Pleiades grows up in a subdued environment where she/he is forced to suppress herself, contain her energy, not show emotions, and constantly conform to her mother. This means that all energy, fire, and power is pressed down and creates profound imbalances in the individual.

The gift of finding one's origin

To find one's origin is to reconnect with our soul and who we are, our true essence. We lift our gaze from our physical body and step into a multidimensional world, a world where anything is possible. We are so much more than what we see with our physical eyes. By understanding who we actually are behind the physical, we become aware of the enormous power we carry and the gifts we have to offer the world.

Each planet and galactic location has its energies and talents and depending on where you come from, you carry these with you as part of your soul constitution. When you know what place, you come from, it can lead to an increased awareness of what you are supposed to do here on earth. Are you here to contribute your high light energy? Are you here to share your amazing communication skills? Perhaps you are here to contribute new and revolutionary technology?

If you are unsure whether you are a Starseed, we can say the following: you who are reading this book and have come this far are most likely a Starseed. Otherwise, you would not have had an attraction to read or know more about the subject.

Some people feel a strong connection to several galactic locations and others to a specific location. If you feel that you have a connection to several places, that's perfectly fine. You can have lived life in multiple places, and it doesn't matter. It just means that you have been and are a traveling soul who enjoys seeing new places. There are several ways to find out which soul group you belong to, and nothing is set in stone. Don't take it too seriously but see it as an exploration where you are open and discover new parts of yourself.

To find out more about your origins, you can read about the different places and see which one resonates most with you, i.e. what feels right. You can also listen to videos about different origins and create an idea of your belonging there. Another way is to contact someone who works specifically with this topic. But remember, in the end it's always up to you to decide what feels right for you.

Right now, there are relatively many Starseeds incarnated on Earth, approximately 20% of the Earth's population. This number will increase in the future as the Earth moves more and more into a collective awakening. Many children born today are Starseeds and you can tell as many of them are very wise even at a young age. They have a great sensitivity and pay attention early on to what is going on in their surroundings. Many of the children who today receive diagnoses of various kinds are, in our opinion, old souls and Starseeds. They are here with an obvious purpose, to teach people to let go of templates for how we should be and live here on earth.

We live in a transformative time where more and more people are waking up, which is very positive. Many are Starseeds who have chosen to come down to earth at this particular time, to contribute their light and to help raise the earth's frequency. Some come here to Earth only once to help, but many Starseeds have lived many lives here on Earth. It has led them into patterns and karma with other people, something that needs to be balanced in this life. As soon as we step down here on earth, we are drawn into what is going on here. This means that balancing karma and imbalances is part of the journey here for many old souls and Starseeds.

As you read the descriptions of soul groups, try to feel the energy behind the words. Don't just read the text but feel the energy behind it. We have selected the most common groups and places that we came into contact with during our work. There are of course more than these groups.

THE PLEIADES

The Pleiades are a star cluster and one of the more common groups we come into contact with. There are relatively many souls from the Pleiades who have chosen to incarnate on earth at this particular time. This is because much of this energy is now needed on Earth. Souls from the Pleiades have a lot of fire in their energy, a lot of power, strength, and creativity. They often have great and well-developed communicative abilities and are well suited to work as self-employed, teachers or something else where they can be free and do their thing. Pleiadean souls have a lot of energy and can be a little restless. They want things to happen quickly and can get impatient when it takes time. It is important that these souls are allowed to express and use all the energy they carry because otherwise they can create a lot of stagnation in the body and thus physical or emotional problems in life.

Souls from the Pleiades can have a strong attraction to areas such as astrology, the stars, and areas of healing and spirituality. Since these souls have a great communicative ability, they are often well suited as leaders or teachers in a field they are really passionate about. It is important that they feel passion for what they do, otherwise they get bored very quickly and lose their focus.

In addition to what we mentioned, they are skilled at transforming external energy, that is, taking external energy into their energy field and transforming it with the help of their strong and high energy. It usually happens unconsciously.

Gifts: Strong drive, fire, passion, strong healing power, strong willpower, intuition.

Challenges: Restlessness, poor patience, difficulty completing things & projects.

SIRIUS

Souls originating from Sirius are organized and thrive in various types of groups or contexts where they can help and provide service. They often enjoy having a project in progress and are well suited to seeing projects through, due to their structured side. Souls from Sirius often have a strong intuition and a lot of healing within them. While Pleiadean souls are more explosive, Sirius souls can be somewhat more reserved with outward emotions. They are perceived as quite safe and as if they have a handle on the situation. Souls from Sirius often have a strong attraction to ancient periods in history such as Ancient Greece or Egypt. They are often drawn to areas such as magic, alternative medicine or other things that go outside the usual healing arts.

Gifts: creativity, spirituality, sensitivity, service oriented, project manager, helpful, fits in groups.

Challenges: Can be a little closed off emotionally, absorbs a lot of external energies.

HADAR

Hadar is or was a star where many souls were "taken over" by a negative or dark soul group. This means that many souls from Hadar in particular carry this with them as a spiritual trauma or memory within them. This trauma has since continued in various forms and here on earth many Hadar souls have experienced very tough things. Souls from Hadar often have many lives behind them with much pain, slavery, oppression, and confinement. It may seem negative, but in the end, it also means a great opportunity for deep transformation – to go from darkness and oppression to power, light and love.

Hadar was a place filled with unconditional love and this also characterizes souls from there. These are souls who have an enormous amount of love within them and who want to help others. There is often a great focus on love and relationships in life here on earth. Hadar souls like to give unlimitedly to other people, which is their great gift but also their challenge at times. It is common for Hadar souls to enter dysfunctional relationships where they put themselves down and elevate others, precisely because they think well of most people. Souls from Hadar carry a lot of healing within them and they have a quick energy, something reminiscent of the energy from the Pleiades. They thrive best when things happen and when they are allowed to be free, develop and surround themselves with love.

Another recurring challenge for Hadar souls is a closed heart, due to many events in past lives and on the planet of origin. Here they may have to work to open this up and start trusting people again. Hadar souls are extremely energetically sensitive and empathic in nature. They have a tendency to sacrifice themselves for others, which rarely leads them in the right direction spiritually and developmentally. This is deep in their DNA and collective cellular memory. They need to break free from this to reach their full potential.

Gifts: Loving, relationship oriented, helpful, strong healing, empathic, empathetic, great power.
Challenges: Codependent, gullible, sacrificial, excessive responsibility for others.

MINTAKA

Souls from Mintaka are extremely helpful, and they have a strong ability to uplift other people. They see the positive in those around them and they can easily put themselves second. If they do sports, they will fight to get ahead, but not at the expense of others. They support their fellow contestants and are rarely the type to speak ill of others.

Souls from Mintaka often have a strong connection to water, something that can be of a more positive or negative nature. Some are drawn to the water and love to be around and in water, while others feel the opposite. They have fears connected with water. Because of this connection to water, some Mintaka souls also have a strong connection with aquatic animals, such as fish, whales, or dolphins. They can also experience that they become calm and receive strong healing when they are in water.

Souls from Mintaka are often intelligent and fit well in helping professions such as doctors, nurses, research, or alternative medicine. They are good with other people, but they are rarely completely controlled by their emotions. They usually find it quite easy to find a balance between thoughts and feelings.

Gifts: helpfulness, seeing the bright in everyone, uplifting, objectivity, supportive, strong relationship with water.

Challenges: Can sometimes have difficulty seeing their own abilities, can have fears around water.

VEGA / LYRA

Souls from Vega originate on the planet Vega in the constellation Lyra. This group is sometimes called the Lyrans. Many souls from this soul group have many earthly lives with them and have a strong connection to Atlantis and Lemuria. Therefore, they may feel drawn to these areas and want to reconnect with its energies.

Vega souls are exploratory in their energy, and they enjoy traveling, seeing new places and discovering things in life. They are often passionate, and it is not unusual for them to work in areas such as music, art, or other creative fields. Once they get hooked on something, they put a lot of time and energy into what they are doing. However, they can easily get bored and like to have new things going on.

Souls from Vega have a high energy and they fit well in professions where they can be among people, spread joy and at the same time help in some way. Because Vegas souls like to be everywhere at once, their energy can sometimes become fragmented. This means that they may have difficulty settling down, finding stability and they may feel rootless. These souls are generally very much in their heads, and this means that they can forget to take care of their body and what is going on emotionally. For this reason, grounding is especially important.

Gifts: lightness, uplifting, creativity, changeable, close to humor and laughter, adventurousness.
Challenges: Can be very "up there", hard to ground and find stability.

BLUEPRINTERS

The Blueprinters are a group of souls who travel around the Universe a lot. They choose to incarnate where a lot of help is needed and where there is a great need to help in development. Blueprinters often come down to earth to transform heavy and dark energy as well as to change and create new templates in society. Templates are another word for programming, beliefs and norms created over a long period of time here on earth. An example of how this can look is Twin Flame relationships, where one purpose of the relationship is to recreate and change templates around how a relationship should look. This means that many Twin Flames who meet have great differences such as different origins, different financial backgrounds, or a large age difference.

Because of the purpose of the Blueprinters, these souls often choose to incarnate into tough and dysfunctional families here on Earth. They do it to be able to contribute their light and help where it is most needed. So, a Blueprinter can, for example, choose to grow up in a family where there is sexual abuse, violence or a lot of chaos while growing up. The purpose here is to become aware of the darkness that is included in the image, begin to heal oneself and transform this heaviness into light. Through this healing process, the person helps to heal family karma and old traumas that have been part of the family line for a long time. There is a transformation of energy at the cellular level, something that can help future generations.

Blueprinter souls often have a lot of strength and power within them. They are ancient complex souls with great spiritual gifts. The challenge for them will be not to get stuck in the darkness they brought with them from growing up, but to learn to manage and master it. Then they can make a huge difference here on earth.

Gifts: Extremely strong souls, strong soul constitution, strong healing abilities, transformation.
Challenges: Can get stuck in heaviness and pain unless they manage to transform it and regain their power.

THE POLE STAR

Souls from the Pole Star incarnates as guides here on earth, and they represent stability and direction. They often have an easier time attuning to lower earth energies unlike souls from the Pleiades or Vega. They have an ability to be more in their lower chakras and are usually relatively grounded and anchored with their body and mother earth.

Souls from the Pole Star fit well in practical professions, above all where they can contribute with service and or more practical help. In relationships, they are loyal, and they are often a safe embrace for their loved ones. They have a lot of sense of responsibility, and they usually finish things they set out to do, for better or for worse. A challenge for these souls can be precisely that they stay too long in situations that they no longer really feel good about, just because they feel obligated to stay. Here they may need to bring more flexibility into their energy and review what they can do to develop and move forward, when the time is right.

Gifts: Stability, guiding light, easy to adapt to the body, loyal, completes things and projects.
Challenges: Can become too "fixed" in their way of life and in energy, stagnation, fixed.

THE ANDROMEDA GALAXY

Souls from the Andromeda Galaxy or Mission Realmers have a strong connection to higher dimensions and above all angels or other beings of light. They have in themselves a very high and fine energy, something that many people around them sense. They fit very well in areas that have to do with healing and nursing.

Andromeda souls are caring by nature, and they easily end up in relationships where they take care of both their partner and other family members, sometimes a little too much. Due to their incredibly caring side, they can get stuck in relationships and take on too much responsibility. For this group of souls, it is important that they get out of things that no longer benefit them on their journey and move towards their own self-realization. Souls from the Andromeda galaxy have strong healing abilities and they often have an attraction specifically to angels or other high beings of light. They can also work with angels in their daily work or through their life task.

Gifts: Caring, sacrificing, high and bright energy, angelic energy, healing abilities, good listener.

Challenges: Can take too much responsibility in relationships, hard to invest in themselves.

ARCTURIANS

Souls from Arcturus are advanced souls, and they are often found in fields such as research, technology, advanced forms of healing, medicine, or architecture. They have a high intelligence and are drawn to challenges where they can make a big difference to humanity and help progress forward in various fields. Arcturians are sensitive and empathetic but can sometimes come across as closed off or detached from their inner selves. They often have difficulty understanding and relating to the physical body here on earth. Many Arcturian souls have strong and well-developed healing abilities. They are structured and good at carrying out different types of projects.

On top of that, these souls are often independent and relatively fearless by themselves.

Not infrequently, they have telepathic abilities and a well-developed communication with higher dimensions.

Gifts: High intelligence, technical, advanced spirituality, healing, may have telepathic abilities.

Challenges: Can be perceived as somewhat cold or withdrawn outwardly, difficult with emotions.

Chapter 3

YOUR LIFE TASK AND SPIRITUAL MISSION ON EARTH

This chapter aims to bring you closer to your Life Task or your spiritual Mission as a Starseed in this life. During our work with Old Souls, highly sensitive and Starseeds, we have seen the great importance of one's life task, for several reasons. For Starseeds there is a strong desire to help and to contribute something special here on earth. We may feel that we want something more than just going to work and then spending our time on the couch in front of comics. That's because we ARE here to do something bigger. As a Starseed, you are here to contribute with your knowledge, your light, and the amazing gifts you carry - no matter in what form it takes place.

Getting in touch with your life task and contributing something here on earth is not only important but a Key for you who are an old soul and a Starseed. Through your Life Task, you reconnect with your soul and with your origin. You step into your role as a Lightworker, and you feel that you are following the plan of your Soul.

For old souls, the lesson is not in learning to give, but in giving in a balanced and directed way. Old souls are often givers by nature, which means that they already give and give of themselves and their energy early on. But we need to learn to give in a way that resonates with ourselves. If we give too much of ourselves, we become drained of our own power. We burn out and we shut ourselves off from the outside world, due to exhaustion.

We often see people who have great gifts and enormous potential, but who cannot cope with life as a whole. They have given of themselves for so long and lost their power along the way.

So how can we give in a balanced way? We need to learn to help and assist with service, without giving away our own power. We do this by setting clear boundaries and working with our integrity. We also need to let go of responsibility for people around us and trust their ability to take care of themselves. We can show that we are there for people around us, but we don't have to take responsibility for them. We don't have to - or rather - we shouldn't bear their pain.

When we find our Life Task and share our gifts, it energizes us. It fills us with energy and joy, which makes us raise our own energy. If we are drained or exhausted by what we do, we need to review our energy balance. We need to look at where we give away too much energy and how we can regain the balance here.

What is our Life Mission?

The concept Life Mission can have many different meanings. When we talk about Life Mission, we are mainly referring to two different parts. Both parts are equally important, and they are connected to each other. When we find the power of these two points, we can achieve miracles, for ourselves but also for other people and our planet as such.

The first part is about reconnecting with our soul and our own energy. As we clear and heal blockages, we are constantly getting closer to our core and essence. It leads us towards our soul and towards our divine light. By getting in touch with our inner light, we can help others do the same. When we are in our power and our inner light, we help heal those around us, just by our existence. This way it's not about doing anything special, but just being in our own energy.

The second part is about finding our life's purpose in the outside, where we can share our specific gifts and talents. As an old soul and Starseed, you have accumulated gifts and talents from many lifetimes but also from other galactic locations. By picking out your unique gifts, you can assist with powerful help here on earth. We sometimes meet people who believe they have no special gifts. But that is not true! Everyone has their unique gifts – you just have to find them and dare to use them. When we have a natural gift within us, we often have a hard time seeing it as a gift. This is precisely because it comes so naturally to us, we see it as a matter of course.

Ask yourself the following question: If I could dream completely freely - what would I do during the day?

If we lift away programming, fears, other people's expectations, and duties - what would you do? That's a good question to start with. Look at what dreams you had as a child or what dreams have recurred throughout your life from time to time.

Common challenges connected with our Life Mission
There are certain challenges connected with one's life mission that often recur and are common to old souls and Starseeds in particular. Read through the descriptions and see if you recognize yourself in one or more of them. If you feel that someone is limiting you a little extra, look at how you can work with that theme in yourself.

Fear of failure

We often see this fear in our work. It's a feeling that most people experience at some point in their lives. In old souls there are often deep and underlying fears of failure. That fear often has its origins back in time, already in previous lives. Many past lives mean many experiences and guaranteed a number of failures. Maybe we have had past lives where we thought we disappointed people or where we thought we failed in what we undertook.

But what does failure really mean? Actually, there is no such thing as failure, at least not from a spiritual perspective. There are only experiences and learning of different kinds. The word failure is a concept we humans created. Thus, it is also us humans who define the word failed. We often think that we fail when we cannot cope with something we have undertaken. We can also feel like a failure when we receive criticism from others, etc.

Here it is important to realize the following: we will always go through moments and stages of "failure" in our life. It is a part of life and through our mistakes we learn more about ourselves. We learn what we don't want and what we actually want in our life.

When it comes to work and life tasks, we will most likely encounter both resistance, obstacles, and various forms of failure before we find our thing. If we choose to start our own business and work as entrepreneurs, failures are part of the journey.

Here we need to work with feelings that appear and act lovingly towards ourselves. Feel free to look at whether you have brought with you a lot of demands and expectations of yourself from home.

Fear of succeeding

This challenge may seem strange, but it is not uncommon for us to feel fear of success at anything in life. As long as we do our stuff casually and follow our established patterns, we feel safe. We know who we are in that role and others know how to relate to us. But once we decide to invest in ourselves and follow our dreams, we are forced to face new parts within us. If you are used to standing in the background and dimming your light, it can be uncomfortable to suddenly take a seat and show yourself to the outside. Many old souls are used to dimming their light. So, when we shine our light in the world around us, we can feel uncomfortable and vulnerable.

Let's say you decide to start a YouTube channel, where you share spiritual information. You feel safe and sure of what you are going to do. You record your videos, and the channel starts to grow quickly. Here, feelings of self-doubt, fear of not being enough or thoughts that you are a fraud, etc. may arise.

We can also liken it to public figures we see in society. The better things go for someone, the more criticism and questioning the person may have to face from those around them. This applies not least in the spiritual sphere, as it is still a subject outside the societal norm.

If you experience fears associated with success, you can examine where they come from. You can also be aware that they will come up but continue to do your projects and what you long for.

We do not realize our Potential

We have been on this track before but choose to highlight it further as it is a great challenge for many old souls. It is also something we have both struggled with during parts of our own life journey.

Many old souls and starseeds diminish themselves and their gifts. It often starts already in childhood, whereas a highly sensitive person you try to fit into the environment you live in. If you are born into a dysfunctional family, it is extremely common for a highly sensitive person to start dimming their light and energy early on. It is partly about protecting oneself, but it is also a way of highlighting someone else (for example, a parent or a sibling).

Many old souls incarnate in difficult family relationships, causing them to lose themselves and their connection with the Divine. This may require some work and we need to become aware of the enormous power and potential we actually carry. Look at all the things you have accomplished in life and try to do it with loving eyes. Look back at your upbringing, everything you've been through and see the power you carry.

Remember; what you feel and experience as heavy is never a true part of you. The true part of you is what feels loving, beautiful, peaceful, and magical. This is because the latter states resonate with you origin energy, your connection with Source.

Limitation from Society

Many of us yearn to create and try new paths in life, but feel limited by society and the structure we live in. This is not surprising, as we are largely shaped by the context we grow up in. There are certain rules and templates we need to relate to in order to fit in as people or fit into the group.

Here it is important to look at whether and how society can limit us on the way to our Life Mission here on earth. Many people dream of working alternatively, regardless of whether it concerns medicine, healing, or another form of health. But as soon as we approach these topics, we often quickly become aware of what applies in society. We must stay within the framework of what society's guidelines say. This is deeply rooted in us. Many of us have had past lives where we went against authority and were thus exposed to danger or exclusion.

In order to find our life mission and realize ourselves, we need to be prepared to dare to go against given templates. We will not find our soul's highest potential by going with the flow of everything that happens. Starseeds are strong leaders in themselves and often need to work on highlighting their inner leadership.

This does not mean that we should break society's laws, but we need to look outside the system that is already established. All the people who create new and great things in the world go far in what they do, precisely because they go their own way and create new things.

Look at what opportunities exist in your life to create what you long for? Where are there limitations from the environment? What can you do to get around these limitations? Are there fears connected with society?

Feelings of guilt
Many old souls experience guilt when they choose to follow their own path. It is usually a sign that you have lived too much for other people or that you have entered into adaptation. We are so used to doing what is expected of us that we feel guilty when we do something for ourselves. Maybe you are a parent and are used to always being there for your children. It can also apply to a partner or a family member.

Because your surroundings are used to having you there, there may be reactions from people around you - making you feel insecure. But remember the following:

- It's never wrong to follow your dreams and realize yourself.
- The more you follow your heart and your guidance, the more you can give to those around you.
- You are not responsible for anyone else's life (only your children under 18).
- Your soul's longing is always the most important thing in your life.

If you feel guilty when you invest in yourself, you can think about where this feeling originates. Have you learned to focus and lay focus on your surroundings?

Fears related to Money

Money is a big topic. There are people who claim that spirituality and money are not connected. In our opinion, it has a very strong connection.

Money is pure Energy, just like everything else in the Universe. Money is neither wrong, ugly, good nor bad. Money just is. It is what we choose to do with our money that creates a positive or negative energy. So, when we use our money to do good, a high energy is created. If we use money to hurt or lower someone, a low energy is created.

Many old souls struggle with their finances, and this can be due to many different factors. There may be health problems or difficulties in having a job, making it difficult to cope financially. There can also be fears connected with money that we received from our parents.

Part of the spiritual journey involves going from Lack to Abundance. It's about relationships and health, but also work and our life's mission. When we live in a sense of lack, we create more lack in our life (based on the law of attraction). If we live in an energy and feeling of abundance, we create more of the same energy. If we grew up in an environment where we experienced a lot of lack, the probability is high that we carry this pattern with us for a long time in our lives. If, on the other hand, we grew up in an environment where we were well off and felt secure in the fact that there was money, we may find it easier to create money as an adult. This does not mean that it is always easy to create and manage money, but it can give us a better premise.

We have seen that old souls easily get stuck in the financial part when they start a business or choose to invest in what they want to do. Maybe you choose to follow your dream job but are paid so little that it becomes difficult to manage financially. It is also easy to end up in a spiral where we work and give everything but get too little in return.

With money, the same universal laws apply as with everything else. We should strive for balance in what we do. We need to see the VALUE in what we do for others and charge for our services. Otherwise, it is practically an impossibility to work with Spirituality or any form of own business in the long run.

Look at what your relationship with money looks like! Does the theme bring up something uncomfortable within you?

Have you learned that money is wrong/ugly? How can you create a life where you actually make money and feel pride in what you do?

How can we find our Life Mission?

To answer this question, we need to bring out our imagination and dare to go beyond what we think is possible. Below are three keys that will guide you towards your Life Mission.

Find something you feel Passionate about

The first step is to find your great passion! If you don't have a passion, it's time to find one. When we do something with pure joy and passion, our heart sings – our frequency rises. Find something that you are passionate about and that awakens your inner joy. When you do something, you feel true passion for, it gives you energy. It energizes you, rather than draining you. If you have difficulty finding something, you can think about what you think you could feel passionate about. Feel free to look back on your life and see if there was a passion for something back in the day.

Something you have a talent for

The second step is about sharing your gifts and talents with the outside world. When we feel passionate about something, we usually also have a pretty easy time with that particular thing. For example, if I feel a great passion for singing, the probability is quite high that I have a somewhat good voice.

Look at your natural talents and where you have your gifts. Maybe you have a strong creative side? Maybe you are good at seeing what other people need? Other examples of gifts could be writing talent, artistry, an ability to think outside the box, energy sensitive or good at communicating on a topic.

Remember; when we are good at something, we often have a hard time seeing it ourselves. Authors can often think that writing a book is easy and believe that it is something that everyone can do. You don't have to be an expert in something, but you can see that there is potential to develop and do something with it.

Keep in mind that we typically develop gifts and talents as we grow up, whether harmonious or dysfunctional. If we had a tough upbringing, it often means that we were more or less forced to develop strong gifts - in the form of sensitivity, healing, and empathic abilities.

Something that is needed in the world

The third step is about finding something that the world needs. You're the best in the world at building clay sculptures, but if there's no need for what you're doing, it's pretty much a waste. You can still engage in clay sculpting as a hobby, but when it comes to our Life Mission, it is always something that is needed in our world around us. It can be service, art, therapy talks, healing, care, or anything else that brings joy or help to people. So, we need to blend our passion, our gifts and bring them out in a way that benefits those around us.

We take an example. We imagine that you love to write, which is your great passion. Throughout your life, you have devoted yourself to writing, both in the form of diaries, half-written books, and various forms of notes. In addition to this, you have a great and passionate interest in psychology and how humans work. Based on this, your life task may involve writing books where you highlight your knowledge and experiences about humans and their inner psychological mechanisms.

To summarize the above three points:
- Find what sparks your passion
- Use your natural talents & developed gifts
- Do something the world needs & where you can make a difference

Light work in different forms

There are many forms of light work that we can do here on earth. Sometimes we feel extra drawn to some kind of work. Nothing is better or more important, but they all have their role in our ascension process here on earth. There is an infinite amount we can do to contribute light and healing here on earth. That is what all forms of light work are about, contributing light, transformation, and expansion for ourselves and for other people.

We will now give some examples of how we can work with light work. This is also something you can use as inspiration to find your Life Mission.

Healing

Healing involves light work in the form of healing and balancing energy. We can work with more general or targeted healing. Examples of more targeted healing are chakra healing, where the focus is on the chakra system in particular. Overall, healing is more connected with people and animals rather than places. The purpose of healing is to restore or balance the energy in any place where there is an imbalance.

Energy work

Energy work is reminiscent of healing but can also target different places, for example buildings. We can work with energy work in different ways and here it is important that we find a way that suits us. There is no single method in healing that is right, but we need to find a method that suits our energy and our soul constitution.

A form of light work here can be about working with the energy in special places where there is a concentrated and strong energy. It can be places that were historically significant or where major events took place. An example of such a place could be Stonehenge in England.

Mediumship

Mediumship is about conveying messages from other dimensions. It can be messages and messages from loved ones who have passed away. Here there is often a well-developed ability to pick up and convey words, thoughts or images that come to one in one's work.

Light keeper

Working as a light keeper is about keeping a high frequency of light in oneself, in order to spread this light to one's surroundings. These are often people who find it relatively easy to keep their energy and frequency high. Sometimes we can come across people who are in their light despite having been through tough things throughout their lives. It is part of their gifts to hold and maintain their energy frequency through challenging periods. Usually, these individuals have healed enough within themselves that they can maintain a stability within themselves.

Transformation of Darkness

This form of light work is slightly different from the above forms and here the very foundation lies in transforming dark and heavy energy into light. We can do that by experiencing a lot of dark energy within ourselves and learning to master and transform it. Some old souls are born into very heavy and dark environments to activate their role as light workers in that way. There they learn to be in and experience a low vibration, something that with awareness and healing work they can learn to transform into high frequencies.

Earth Guide

We see this form of light work in individuals who break free from societal norms and who follow their own path through life. They are people who dare to take the lead and show others the way, through the courage to follow their truth. When we dare to go against the flow and follow what we believe in, even though we risk being outside society - then we can make a big difference for many people in society. It doesn't have to be such drastic things as excluding oneself from society, but it's about creating new things and breaking norms.

Mediator of information

This is a form of light work that can express itself in many ways. It is about spreading information to people, through, for example, the media, books, conversations or learning of various kinds. Some people feel strongly that they are here to convey something and wake people up through their words. Today we live in a media society where we have many channels we can use to reach out with our messages. We can make videos on YouTube, write a blog, or use some other forum where we reach larger groups of people. It is common for souls with a strong connection to the Pleiades to be drawn to this type of lightwork.

The importance of bringing our Energy into what we do
Whatever you choose to do - find your unique way of doing it. There are thousands of people who work in healing and there are just as many who engage in mediumship or writing. Whatever you choose to devote your time to, be sure to put your own touch and energy into it. This is an important key, and it depends on the following; when we do something based on our own energy, we attract the right clients and situations that match our energy frequency.

So, let's say you choose to start a business with a spiritual focus. Look closely at how you can make your services unique. What makes people choose your services? What can you contribute based on your unique experiences in life? Find a unique direction and don't underestimate what you can do here on earth.

Chapter 4

WORKING WITH YOUR INTUITION

In this chapter we will delve into intuition, which is our most important tool on our spiritual journey and in our ascension. Without our intuition, we easily get lost and fall into limitation. Our intuition is always there but sometimes we don't hear it. It can be due to external distractions or that there are obstacles blocking. When we are small, we often have good contact with our intuition, and we are open to our inner guidance. But as time goes by, we start to shut down and stop listening to our inner voice, due to conforming to the voices around us and the truth that is assigned to us through life.

Sometimes it is easy to forget how shaped we are by the world we grow up in. As children, we are completely open and receptive to what we hear, experience, and see around us. This means that what surrounds us growing up also becomes our truth and our identity. Imagine that you had grown up in a completely different family, in another country or in another part of the world. Your life would probably have looked completely different, both regarding habits, thoughts, and attitudes.

BUT it is important to know that we always carry with us our inner core, our soul and who we really are. It is the core we need to find our way back to in adulthood. We need to peel off and peel away all that has been put on us in the form of other people's opinions and belief systems. An example of this is school and our school time. For many, school goes on for most of their growing up, which means that we are strongly shaped by its environment. We learn which topics are important, what is important to get involved in, what we should think and think about things in society and so on. In the same way, we are shaped by the family we live with during childhood. We learn which emotions are okay and which emotions we should push away. We learn what we are like and what we are capable of through the reflection of our parents. If our parents have high demands on us, we will develop high demands on ourselves when we get older. With all that said - a big part of our spiritual journey is about freeing ourselves from what we've been taught and getting back in touch with our intuition.

What is our intuition?

Our intuition is our connection with our higher self, our soul, and our guides in higher dimensions. The guidance that takes place through your intuition is always non-judgmental, loving and it guides you towards development and towards your truth. It guides you into your life's path and into your life's purpose. We have different ways of receiving guidance through our intuition and it is important that you find your way. Some receive words and sentences, some see images or symbols, while others only know things within themselves. The more you learn to decipher your own intuition, the easier it is for you to work with this. Quite often we have one or two ways that we work with the most, but we can also have all senses highly developed.

Our 5 most common ways to receive information are:

- **Spiritual hearing** - We hear and perceive inner messages. Messages can come to us as thoughts, sentences, and words. Some hear it more like an external voice, but many perceive the guidance that comes through their own voice, much like we are thinking. Here we may need to learn to tell the difference.

- **Spiritual seeing** - We see symbols, signs, or images in our interior. We can get an image of a situation or different memories that show us something about a situation. Some people get the whole scenario of events while some can get a quick picture of something. This can happen in the waking state but also in the form of symbols and images in our dreams.

- **Spiritual knowing** - We only know things within ourselves, without being sure how we know it. You might meet a person and just know right away that that person will have an important role in your life. Perhaps you read a text and immediately know within yourself that what is written in the text is true.

- **Spiritual sensing** - We sense and sense other people's energies. This means that we can sense what problems someone has and thus get information that way. We may also sense and receive information energetically about a certain place. We can sense the mood when we walk into a room, and we sense that a person is angry, sad, worried, or happy.

- **Spiritual feeling** - This means that we take up other people's emotional states, for example other people's pain, suffering, joy, or sadness. We experience and take these feelings into our body as if they were our own feelings. Let's say you hang out with a close friend who is sad. Suddenly your heart aches and you feel heaviness inside. You have picked up the other person's feeling and feel it in your body.

We can also use our sense of smell and taste to receive information, but the five ways mentioned above are the most common that we use.

How can we distinguish our ego from our intuition?
After time and solid work with ourselves, we learn to distinguish between our intuition and our ego. It often takes a period of inner work and reflection to get here. Below are some important basic principles that you can relate to in your everyday life.

The ego keeps you in the comfortable and ingrained
The ego does not want to develop
The ego cherishes physical safety
The ego repeats patterns, rather than entering into new ones
The ego often expresses words such as never or always

Your intuition guides you into the unknown
Your intuition guides you towards your passion
Your intuition makes you break patterns
Your intuition guides you towards new challenges
Your intuition never speaks judgmentally

The intuition and influence of Darkness

Many of you who read this book have strong experiences connected with spirituality in past lives. Perhaps you worked as a Healer or some kind of Light worker in a previous life or in another place. We humans are often drawn to that which is an important part for us and which we are familiar with in one way or another.

Together, we have had thousands of sessions with people and when we have explored their past lives with them, there is always an element of spirituality in some form. It is something amazing and it means that many times we just continue where we left off in previous lifetimes. The challenging part here is about the darkness and the fears many people feel connected to particular events in past lives. This is something we see over and over again in our work. We have also done extensive cleansing work in ourselves, where we healed heavy parts from past lives.

In many parts of the world, we live in a relatively open climate, even if spirituality in particular is still somewhat hushed up and taboo. Imagine a life back in history, were many people learned the hard way that spirituality was not allowed to be practiced. At worst, we were punished or killed because of our faith, unless it went hand in hand with Christianity (an example). As we return to later in the book, our past lives have a major impact on our lives today, because we are energetic beings and because time does not really exist in linear form. Many of the deep fears and limitations we carry today have their origins in our past lifetimes. We see it clearly in our client conversations. We see individuals who decide to work in the spiritual realm and as soon as they start their business, it stops. Many experience it practically as a wall, as if they are doing wrong or as if something is preventing them from moving forward. Here it is common that we have deep fears or different types of dark energies that affect us. It can sometimes be difficult to get a handle on this because we don't remember the original event itself associated with the fear we feel.

Further on in the book, you will find a separate chapter specifically on dark energy and how we can work in-depth with it. Here and now, we want to advise you to clear your intuition and connection when you need to feel something, if you feel that it is difficult to get answers or if it feels blocked. You can do that by, for example, expressing the following before you work on something:

"I ask Archangel Michael and my highest guide team to help me clear my connection and my intuition completely. Clear all forms of negative or dark energy. I am asking to receive the highest purest guidance that resonates with my higher self and my highest truth right now. Thanks"

Remember that there is never a right or wrong when asking for help or working with the spiritual. Your intention is the important thing, the rest you can post as you wish. What we cover are tips and advice.

How can you work with your intuition?
We will now give you some exercises that you can use to train your intuition. Remember that practice makes perfect and the more you practice, the more confident you become in what you achieve. This bears repeating because we've noticed that many people give up when things don't work out at first and tell themselves they can't. Intuition cannot disappear, nor can it be damaged, but there may be

things that are temporarily obscured. The more you work with the shadow, the closer you get to your intuition.

To strengthen the connection with your inner self, always set a clear intention before you work with a certain exercise or feel something. By setting an intention, you create clarity both for yourself and for the Universe about what you want to do. It also becomes a clear direction within yourself, that you actually WANT to make a change. An intention can be: "I now choose to work with my fear of flying and let my intuition guide me through this!"

Exercise 1

1. Sit comfortably and take a few deep breaths.
2. Choose a topic you want to work on, for example internal stress.
3. Ask your intuition at what age this stress started and see what comes to you. Uncertainty may arise here but just see what comes to you. You can't go wrong, but it's a matter of testing yourself and eventually you'll learn this more and more. Let's say you reach the age of 7. It could also be that you get a certain event, or you see the first day when you start school. Then these are events and pictures that show you that you were around 7 years old.
4. Then ask for information about what happened then. Trust what comes to you here! You might recall a memory, a feeling, a situation or just a recollection of something. Everything is okay!
5. By accessing a feeling, thought or image of the event, the energy will come up that is connected to this very thing. The energy

that was locked and that created blockages in connection with what happened.

6. If one or more feelings come up, allow yourself to feel the feelings as much as possible. Remember that emotions are pure energy and completely harmless. It can also be a more ongoing feeling such as general anxiety. Then do the same and ask where it comes from. Then you may realize that you were not seen in childhood or that your mother was emotionally unstable, which created an inner insecurity for you.

7. This is often enough to start an inner healing process and find things that we need to heal. Feel free to take a moment a day where you ask one or more questions and work with what comes up.

Exercise 2

1. Sit or lie down comfortably and take a few deep breaths.

2. Choose a topic you want to work on or just get a feel for what you're going to work on. Let's say you choose anger.

3. Ask if the anger originated in this or a past life and trust the first thing that comes up. In this case we say it comes from past lives.

4. Imagine that you are entering the Intuition Cloud, a fluffy white cloud where all your past experiences are gathered - both positive and negative. If you want, you can visualize yourself entering this cloud or you can just know it within yourself.

5. Ask your intuition to give you the information you need to be able to work on the topic you have chosen.

6. You are in this cloud and pay attention to what is coming to you. Maybe you get a country, a year, a color, a smell, a memory, or a feeling.

7. Ask questions like – Where am I? Am I a man? Woman? What happens? What do I feel? Do I have another person there?

8. Trust that what comes up is relevant to what you need to know.

9. This helps to rekindle and bring to light the root event of the problem you are experiencing. Maybe you bring up a past life in America where you were a native Indian and were the victim of an assault. Or maybe it just comes up that it's a different country and you were exposed to something that caused fear and anger. It is enough! The energy locked up here will now begin to release and you will heal. We don't always need to get so much information, but it is the healing itself that we want to access.

If you want to enhance the healing, you can ask your higher self to help you heal and release the cellular memory associated with the event. Trust that the healing is happening, regardless of whether you feel it strongly in the moment or not! When you really have an intention to heal, it will always happen.

If your ego kicks in or you start to doubt, take a few deep breaths, and just relax. Release all pressure on yourself and try to find a playfulness in it. Find an exploratory rather than judgmental approach. Here you need to be patient with yourself and the process.

Chapter 5

WORKING WITH A PENDULUM

In this chapter we will delve into how you can use the pendulum in your healing work. Working with the pendulum is an amazing tool and if we learn to use it correctly, it can help us access deep parts within ourselves and find unconscious aspects. Some can sense things directly through their intuition, but sometimes we may need a tool to really reach things within us. You can use the pendulum in larger parts of your work or combine it with sensing things freely. The more we use the pendulum, the more our intuition tends to develop as well. So, after some time with the pendulum, you may feel in and know the answer even before the pendulum shows you an answer.

Many clients we have come into contact with have tried the pendulum, but feel that it does not work, that it is unclear or that they do not really know how to use it. The prerequisite for getting ahead and getting the most out of a pendulum is to use it correctly. This does not mean that there is only one way of working, but we need to be sure of what we do and how we do it. Otherwise, we easily end up in doubt and put the pendulum away.

The pendulum itself has no wisdom or knowledge, but the answers we get through the pendulum come from our intuition, our higher self, and our higher guides - IF we choose to take help from there. When it comes to spiritual work, it is very important that we have a clear intention with what we want. So, in this case it is important that you connect the pendulum to the person or thing you wish to receive an answer from. Otherwise, it becomes unclear, and the answers can actually come from anything. What we want to use the pendulum for is to get answers from our intuition or some higher light guide.

How to set the Pendulum

Feel free to buy a pendulum with a clear tip at the bottom as it makes it easier if you are going to use charts and get answers. If you already have a pendulum, it is of course fine to use it. The pendulum itself has no magical powers, but is an extension of our intuition, a tool for eliciting answers. In order to use the pendulum, you need to set it up so that you know what it responds to.

What you need to set is:

- A Yes
- A No
- A Maybe/Unclear

To set these responses, you can hold up the pendulum using your thumb and forefinger (find a way that works for you). Then do the following:

1. Ask the pendulum to show you a yes! The pendulum will here start to move in one direction
2. Ask the pendulum to show you a no! The pendulum must here move in a different direction
3. Ask pendulum to show you a maybe/unclear

When you have obtained these, the setting is complete and then these always apply as answers. Don't start changing the answers but keep the first ones that come, otherwise it can get confusing. If you don't get an answer, ask the pendulum again to show you an answer until you have a clear answer for all three. The movements don't have to be that big, but it's enough that you can distinguish what it is.

Create a higher connection

Now find a way to connect with your intuition, higher self, or guides. Choose what suits you. This is a way to connect the pendulum with higher guidance, so you know where the answers are coming from. Feel free to do this every time you use the pendulum. Suggestions for what you can say are:

"I now choose to connect with my higher self, archangels, and ascended masters in the fifth dimension and higher, for guidance and direction. I ask to receive only those answers that resonate with my highest life path and my highest good right now."

This is also a good and easy way to enter a higher energy - you set a clear intention with what you want to do. Be aware that you don't have to say the exact words above, but the important thing is the intention for what you want. Dare to find the words that suit you and trust that everything will happen.

Clear the pendulum

We usually clear the pendulum before using it as we have noticed that outside energies can interfere and affect the responses sometimes. So, find a way to clear the energy for the pendulum. Here Archangel Michael is good to take help of because he works a lot with releasing and clearing. A sign that we may need to cleanse is that the pendulum gives unclear answers or that it behaves a little strangely. You will learn to notice this if you use the pendulum for a while. For example, you could say something like:

"I ask Archangel Michael to cleanse the pendulum so that it is completely clean and embedded in light. Clear out all lower, negative, and dark energies that may affect the answers. I also ask for help to clear my energy so that it is pure and to lift out the ego and fears."

Trust that this helps, and should you notice during your work that the pendulum starts to behave a bit strangely or that you get a lot of double messages, feel free to cleanse further. If you find that it doesn't help, keep cleansing until you notice relief. The further we get in our work and the bigger things we access in our interior, the more we can notice that the pendulum is affected. It can be affected by both our own fears, external energies, and other things. It is important here that you constantly go back into your power and know that it is YOU who has the power. Don't be afraid of the pendulum or that it will be affected but try to find security in this.

How can you work with the pendulum?
You can use the pendulum to ask questions about your inner self and feel free to ask follow-up questions on what you find out. The more we get down to the level of detail, the better for what we are going to clear and heal.

An example of how you can work:

- Do I have a blockage in the heart chakra? (let's say you get a Yes)
- Did the blockage occur in this life? (No)
- Did it occur in a previous life? (Yes)
- Was I a woman in that life? (Yes)
- Was it in Europe? (No)
- Was it in Asia? (Yes)
- Did something happen in that life that is connected with the heart? (Yes)
- Was I exposed to something? (Yes)
- Does it have to do with a man? (Yes)
- Was it a man I had a relationship with? (Yes)
- Did he rape me? (No)
- Violence? (Yes)
- Was I afraid of him? (Yes)
- Did this create a blockage in the heart? (Yes)

The text above shows that the blockage comes from a past life where you were a woman living in Asia. You lived with a man who subjected you to violence and you were afraid of him. This energy created a blockage in your heart. Once you find this information, you can ask your higher self and your guides for help to heal the cellular memory from that life and release the blocked energy. Emotions or memories may come up, but not always. Trust that you are getting the information you need and ask for help to let this go!

So, you can use the pendulum to get information about different things, but you can also use the pendulum to confirm things you sense with your intuition. Let's say you sit down and ask questions. You feel in intuitively and get a few different things. If you want to know if what you have picked up is correct, you can use the pendulum to confirm the information. You may discover that you have a trauma from childhood, something that happened when you were three years old. You get an image of losing your mother. If you feel unsure if it is your intuition speaking to you, ask the pendulum; Is the information I received, correct?

Another way you can use the pendulum is to use charts. You can either make slightly more advanced charts on a computer or draw your own charts. Here, the only limit is your imagination and creativity.

If you want to make a chart on your own, take a white paper and put it in front of you. Let's say you choose to work on understanding your inner anxiety. Draw a smaller circle in the middle where you suggest writing Worry. Then draw several different lines based on the circle in the middle so that it looks like a sun. You can choose how many lines you want. At the end of each line, write down different options for what your concern could be. It can be things like childhood, previous life, event at work, something unconscious or several reasons, etc. Then set your pendulum and hold it in the center above the circle. Then ask where does my anxiety come from? Your pendulum will then start to move and show what is the cause. If it doesn't, ask the question again until you get an answer. This is how you can do with several different things and try to do it in a way that feels good to you.

You can also make an emotion chart where you do the same, so you find out which unconscious emotions you need to work with right now. Then you write down different emotions on the chart and ask your question, for example "Which unconscious emotion do I need to work with right now?"

Charts are a very good and powerful way to find unconscious things within us, which affect us a lot.

You don't have to worry about influencing the pendulum to respond in a certain way. Ask questions and try to be as neutral as possible about the question - be open to whatever answer comes. If you notice that it is unclear, go back and cleanse the pendulum again. Find the curiosity within you and see this as something developing and exciting, rather than something you have to do.

We also want to emphasize the following - YOU have control and power over the pendulum, not the other way around. The pendulum is just an extension of your inner self so it can't do anything strange or dangerous in any way.

Chapter 6

WORKING WITH LIGHT GUIDES

We use a lot of help and support from higher guides in our work, and it has given us a tremendous amount of support, healing and insights on our journey. In this chapter, we highlight how you can work with different types of light guides and what their different energy qualities are.

Why take help from higher Light Guides?
We all have higher guides with us, and some guides stay with us for life, while others come and go. This is because we need more help and support in certain specific periods of life. When we undergo major changes and inner development, we always have extra support from higher dimensions and from our guides. Taking help from our guides can make it easier for us to move through challenges and to release and heal things that limit us. They are a great gift available to us during our time on earth and they long to guide and support us on our journey.

As we undergo an awakening or move further into our spiritual ascension, it can sometimes create a lot of fear and chaos within us. We may have to face our own darkness and what holds us back. By darkness, in this case, we mean things that you have inside you but are still unconscious - fears, ideas about yourself or feelings that you don't want/can't feel. As long as something is in uncertainty, it remains something heavy/dark and we have no way to look at it or change it. It is only when we allow things to come to the surface and be made aware that we can create something positive from them. We can transform darkness into light by facing it. While going through these processes, we can feel alone, overwhelmed, and insecure. This is natural and one thing we have learned through meetings with many people and not least in meeting each other; we can have people around us, but we need to make our inner journey on our own. It does not always mean that we are alone on the outside, but it means that no one can fully understand what we are going through. Our inner journey and our life path are divine, and it is between us and the Universe.

Here it can be absolutely fantastic to reach out a hand and ask our guides and angels for help. They are there all the time but since we have free will here on earth they cannot intervene in any way without our permission. We need to express what we want help with, where we want to go and what our longing is. This is where our intention comes in, which we previously talked about. If we don't know what we want ourselves, how are the guides supposed to know?

Angels, Archangels and Ascended Masters all have unique energetic properties which allow them to help us in different ways. Some work more on releasing old while others help bring new energy into our energy bodies and replenish with power. The more we work with one or certain guides, the more we will get to know their energy, and, in the end, we can often feel when they are with us and that they help us in various contexts.

To receive help from higher Guides
Working with higher guides is actually very easy because it is something natural for us, for our soul. You don't need to have any

special formula or express yourself in the right way, all you need to do is the following:

- Ask for help and express what you want help with.
- Allow help to come through trust! By having trust, we open up for the flow to come through.
- Be open to help coming in the form it is meant to. Let go of notions that it should happen in a certain way.
- Thanks for the help!

It might sound like this:

"I ask Archangel Michael for help to let go of old things that hold me back. I am ready to let go of what limits me! I trust that I will get the help I need. Thanks for any help!"

Or like this:

"I ask you, Mary Magdalene, to help me heal my heart. Help me heal blockages and heavy feelings in my heart. I pray for healing for my pain!"

Find a way that feels good to you and remember that everything we write is support and encouragement rather than directives. There is no right or wrong in spiritual work, but your intention guides your work. We will now cover a range of archangels, ascended masters, and goddesses that you can use in your work. You can choose to work with one or more in different contexts. As soon as you call upon them and trust them to be there, they will BE there with you. There are of course more than these to work with, but we have selected those that we have noticed are powerful and that often show up for us on our spiritual path.

Archangel Michael

Archangel Michael is a powerful angel and guide who helps and supports many light workers around the world. He helps clear negative and fear-based energy and release the old in various aspects of your life. With his sword, he can cut negative energy strings to other people, souls and places that limit you. You can use him to clear your energy system, your aura, your chakras and to clear things that disturb your intuition or pendulum. He is also a powerful protector so you can ask for his protection in various contexts.

Archangel Gabriel

Archangel Gabriel is an angel who helps you with your expression and communication. Feel free to ask for his help if you want to improve your communication with guides or with other people. He helps you clear away things that prevent your communication from flowing freely and smoothly. This is also strongly connected to the throat chakra and your inner truth. You can ask him for help to clear the throat chakra and open up the chakra for better and clearer communication.

Archangel Raphael

Archangel Raphael is an angel with strong healing abilities, and he helps you heal your physical body. You can ask him for help if you have physical pain, illness or inner anxiety and stress in your body.

You can also ask him to help you balance your organs and your physical body in general.

Archangel Vywamus

Archangel Vywamus helps you expand and balance your energy system as well as strengthen your connection to the Universe and your connection to Mother Earth. You can ask for his help to upgrade your energy system and to repair your cells and DNA. Feel free to do this as part of your daily routine, so that the energy flows through your chakras and your body.

Archangel Sandalphom

Archangel Sandalphom helps you with your grounding so that you feel more stable and more in touch with yourself and Mother Earth. Feel free to ask him for help if you feel stressed, confused, lost or ungrounded. At the same time, please imagine roots going down from the center of the earth, up through the ground, through your feet, legs and all the way up to the root chakra. Trust that it will happen!

Metatron

Metatron helps you with your inner power and strength. Ask Him to strengthen you inside and to fill you with more strength when you feel weak or insecure. His energy supports you and builds your inner strength and self-esteem.

Lords of Karma

The Lords of Karma have insight into your Akashic records, which is your spiritual archive. They have knowledge and control of all your soul connections, agreements, and contracts with other souls. You can ask these to help you clear things from past lives, such as old karma, negativity or soul contracts that no longer serve your highest good. We often use these together with Archangel Michael when we work with clearing things from past lives as it becomes very powerful.

Jesus

Jesus was a powerful healer when he lived on earth, and he helped people heal pain and anxiety. He contributed love, compassion, and forgiveness. Jesus' energy helps you with self-love, acceptance, compassion and forgiveness. Ask him for help to heal what is unhealed within you. If you have high demands on yourself or find it difficult to forgive yourself or someone else, he will help you with this.

Mary Magdalene

Mary Magdalene is Jesus' Twin Flame and together they symbolize Yin & Yang – the masculine and feminine within us. She stands for the feminine power and helps you, among other things, to heal imbalances in relationships and intimacy or sexual abuse from this and previous lives. She also helps balance and bring in more of your feminine power. If you are very much in your masculine energy (thought, analysis, activity, practice), then you can ask Mary Magdalene to highlight your feminine qualities and its energy more in your life.

Goddess Kuan Yin

Kuan Yin is a powerful goddess who helps you heal and upgrade your inner child. Ask her for help to heal childhood trauma and inner pain from past events. Kuan Yin has a very caring and motherly energy, so feel free to use her if you want to bring in more self-love and take more care of your inner self. An important goddess for you who are on a deeper inner journey and consciously healing your inner child.

Goddess Lady Nada

Goddess Lady Nada helps you heal and open the heart. Maybe you have major blockages in your heart or a closed heart due to various events. Ask for her help to open up and balance the heart. Lady Nada also helps to strengthen you in your relationships, for example with your Twin Flame or in some other spiritual relationship. Ask for her help to clear the energy between you, to remove old karma and to strengthen the relationship between you and your partner.

Goddess Kali

Goddess Kali helps clear dense and very negative energies. You can use her help together with Archangel Michael if you notice that there is a lot of energy coming in or affecting you negatively. You can also ask her for help in clearing lower guides, other souls, or darkness of various kinds. If you use a pendulum and find it difficult to remove external energies, you can ask the help of her and Archangel Michael to clear a little more deeply.

The Pleiades

The Pleiades and their amazing energy stand for change, power, manifestation, and inspiration. If you feel that you want to move forward or that you are standing and stomping, you can ask for this energy to come in and push you forward, to inspire you and create new things. Souls from the Pleiades are often very creative and love development and change. Ask for their help to move forward and they will guide you.

Arcturians

Arcturians are highly developed light guides, and they contribute a lot of protection to the earth in the time we live in. Ask for their help when you experience a lot of darkness, fear, or anything else that limits you. If you feel that you have a lot of energy around you or within you in general, you can take help from these guides.

Universe & The higher Source

You can also choose to work directly with the Universe and the highest Source if it feels right for you. You are part of the Universe and the source of wisdom that is all around us. Ask the Universe to show you the next step you need to take to help with healing or to get information about something.

The Galactic Center

The Galactic Center acts as a guardian, a kind of Gatekeeper between our and other Galaxies. Many starseeds have unconscious or conscious contact with the Galactic Center and they can help us come more into our life purpose here on Earth. They have a council called the Galactic Council, which deals with what is happening here on Earth. They keep negativity and darkness from spreading to other galaxies, just as they keep negativity from other galaxies from reaching Earth. You can ask the Galactic Council to help you reconnect more with your original starseed energy and to gain more access to your gifts. Often, as a Starseed, you have been involved in this council between your incarnations. In addition to this, the Galactic Council works to make positive changes for us at the cell and DNA level, so that we collectively raise our consciousness and our vibration on Earth.

Chapter 7

RESISTANCE AND OBSTACLES
ON THE WAY

Sooner or later, you will most likely encounter resistance in your inner work. The reason we know this is because we ourselves have had to face and deal with an enormous amount of resistance within ourselves. It is part of the journey and when we dare to do things and move forward DESPITE this, magical things happen within us and in our life. We take ourselves to new levels and develop. Every time we take ourselves to a new level, we need to face new parts of ourselves, things we have not fully understood or integrated within ourselves. When we solve that piece of the puzzle within us, we move on. This is what is called development, and it will always be uncomfortable and difficult, until we find the key and can move on.

Spiritual development is not so much about being positive but about constantly challenging yourself and facing your fears. Without that piece, we won't get very far, because we let fear stop us. Allow yourself to be afraid and give yourself acceptance and love. But then take the plunge and move on, at least a little bit.

When it comes to intuition, it often works well as long as we feel in a little simpler things in everyday life such as which way to take the car or which food is good for us. But when we get down to the depths of our inner self and above all when we begin to approach our deepest wounds, then the intuition can feel unclear, and it feels as if we are groping in the dark. Just because it gets blurry doesn't mean the intuition isn't there, rather the opposite. The blurrier and vaguer it is, the more likely you are on the right track. Nor do we always need to get everything, every detail. If we bring up a thought, a feeling, or an image, it is often enough for us to be able to dissolve and release the blockage. The more you let go of the idea of how it should be or that you have to get things in a certain way or in a certain amount, the easier the information flows to you.

If you're working with your intuition or pendulum and notice it's getting shaky, you can always ask for help. Ask your guide team for help to clear heavy energies that interfere, to lift away your ego and fears and to receive clear guidance. For example, it could sound like this:

"I ask my higher guides to clear energies that negatively affect my intuition and to lift away my ego and fear-based energies that hinder me in my process! Cleanse everything that prevents me from receiving high and pure guidance. Cleanse deeply, in each chakra and at the cellular level"

Trust that you will get the help you need and try again. This usually gets easier and easier over time. We cannot emphasize enough how important your TRUST is in these processes. Trust what you get and trust that you will get help. When you are in trust, you allow things to come to you – you open yourself up to receiving flow and information. If you notice that it's getting very heavy, you can ask your higher self, the guides, or the Universe for help to clear your entire energy system of everything that shouldn't be there.

In addition to this, you can examine what comes up within you. If you notice that nothing happens even though you cleanse and try again, it may be that there are certain things inside you that make it difficult for you. We may have blockages in the third eye and crown chakra that make it difficult for information to reach. Ask for help to clear energy in these chakras that are affecting you negatively.

We can also have feelings within us that we need to face. If you notice that it is difficult to get in touch with your inner self, then start looking at how you can work to get closer to yourself. Are there fears about getting things? Are you afraid of what will come up? Be honest with yourself here! It is common that we want information but at the same time feel a certain resistance or fear about what we are going to get. That's totally fine! Go into the feelings that come up whether it's fear of what you're going to do feeling or fear of feeling nothing. Face the feelings, face the fear. When you do that, you get past the barriers you've built up within yourself. Remember to test yourself and try to find a loving approach to yourself! Be your own teacher rather than judging or blaming yourself. Then the process will go faster and smoother.

So, in summary:

- Ask your higher self or your guides to clear away any distractions.
- Ask for help to clear and balance the third eye and crown chakra.
- Watch and examine the emotions that come up, such as doubt or fear.
- Have confidence that you will receive guidance and the necessary help.
- Trust opens up things to come to you.
- Dare to face and go through your fears.

PART 2

BLOCKAGES & HEALING

Chapter 8

OUR DIVINE AND COMPLEX
CHAKRA SYSTEM

Our chakras are the very foundation of our energy system, and they
make up a large part of our energy body. Most of us know that we
need to take care of our physical bodies – eat well, exercise, rest, sleep
well, etc. But many of us fail to take care of our inner self and our
chakras. It is not so strange, since we do not see them in the physical.
Taking care of our chakras and ensuring that the life energy flows
optimally is not only important, but in our opinion a prerequisite for
being able to live the life our soul longs for. It is our chakras that keep
us healthy, that provide us with life energy and that allow us to live,
create and manifest in life.

How does Energy flow through our Chakras?
Our chakras work together with our meridian system which can be
likened to an energetic network within us. We have 12 main
meridians, and they help transport energy (life energy) from our
chakras out to different parts of our body. They reach out to and
encompass all our important organs and different systems in the
body - and ensure that energy flows freely. When energy flows freely
through our meridians and out into our organs, we stay healthy and
balanced. We experience flow and things feel simple and obvious.
The energy gets from a chakra to our meridians via something called
Nadis (smaller energy channels) in Eastern philosophy.

Each chakra has the ability to capture, store and release energy. In the meeting with other people, an energetic exchange takes place, and our chakras capture the energy. If the energy is managed and processed optimally in the chakra, it flows in a way that makes us feel calm and well. Any energy that is blocked or stuck in a chakra will affect us in one way or another and eventually manifest as some form of imbalance, illness and so on.

What is stored in our Chakras?

Our chakras store energy from past experiences, memories, feelings, and thoughts. This in turn affects the way we look at things, how we feel and how we act. To create new, we need to heal and transform the old that keeps us in the same old pattern.

In each chakra there is also stored energy and information from previous lives and from the time in the mother's womb. Every time we leave our body here on earth, we take with us all the energy that is in our etheric body. When we are then born in a new body, this energy comes with it, which means that in this life we may have to work with a trauma from a previous life. It may seem negative, but it means we get a new opportunity to free ourselves from that trauma and heal. For that reason, many old souls have a lot to heal from past lives and thus may need to do deep work and healing in their chakras.

It is not only blockages and traumas that are stored in our chakras but also our gifts, talents and what we have learned over lifetimes. So, let's say you are working on healing in your chakras. You work with your lower chakras and then you move upwards where you clear and heal in your Third Eye. Our Third Eye stands for Intuition and inner vision. The chakra thus also contains the energy and the gifts that have to do with that area. So, when you work through the chakra and heal blockages, you also come into contact with these gifts, such as clairvoyance.

However, it is important to know that all the chakras are connected and often we need to start with our lower chakras to access and open up more in our higher chakras.

How are Blockages created in our Chakras?

Our chakras react to and take in what we experience in the environment, and this starts with our first breath. Depending on what we have around us and how open/sensitive we are to what is happening, our chakras will react. If we grow up in an environment where there is a lot of love, security, and calmness, that is the energy that enters our chakras. Our chakras will then react in a positive way and the energy will flow as it should. We become confident in ourselves, learn how to build relationships, and build a good foundation to stand on.

If we have a very stressful upbringing where we constantly experience threats, scary things, conflicts, or insecurity, it will affect our chakras very negatively. When we experience strong anxiety or stress for a long time or when we go through something traumatic, it becomes difficult for our chakras to take in, process and release the energy in a positive way. The energy is stopped, remains in the chakra and the flow decreases. This leads to a blockage in the flow of energy. If this goes on for a long time, it can lead to the entire chakra being damaged and almost completely blocked.

A blocked chakra means that the energy does not flow as it should, neither in nor out through the chakra. This in turn means that we also do not get life energy or positive energy into the chakra. Instead, stagnation is created where the chakra is filled with locked energy and unprocessed emotions. This energy affects related organs in the body and in severe cases it can lead to serious diseases and mental illness. In addition to the energy affecting our body, it also functions as part of our overall energy, which we then attract and manifest from. If we then have a large unprocessed trauma in the Sacral Chakra, that energy attracts things and circumstances that match its energetic vibration - Like attracts like according to the law of attraction. Everyone is different and how an external event affects one of your chakras will differ. The more energy sensitive you are, the more you can be affected.

A chakra can become blocked in two different ways, and this means that a chakra can be either underactive or overactive. Depending on which it is, it will affect the chakra and your existence in slightly different ways. Sometimes the energy flows too little in the chakra and other times the energy is too intense. In both cases there is an imbalance in the chakra.

Underactivity in the Chakra

When we write about blockages in our chakras, it is usually this type of imbalance that we are referring to. Underactivity means that the energy in a chakra is limited or blocked. It is blocked and thus cannot flow as it should. You can also say that the chakra is closed. An example of an underactive Solar plexus chakra is when we have difficulty being ourselves, difficulty taking our place and being in our power. When it comes to these types of blockages, we need to make sure to heal and process what is in the chakra and get the flow of energy going. If we have many blockages in a chakra, we may need to take a layer at a time.

Overactivity in the Chakra

When a chakra is overactive, it means that the energy is at high speed in the chakra, that the energy flow is rushing. You can also say that the chakra is too open. It leads to a "speeded up" chakra and an example of an overactive Solar plexus chakra is when we take up too much space, constantly have to be in the center or emphasize our needs and our power in an excessively dominant way. If we take this imbalance to its extreme, we see the well-known narcissist who constantly acts based on himself and his needs. However, not all imbalances are close to narcissism.

An overactive chakra is often a compensation for something within ourselves or someone close to us, for example our mother. Let's say your grandmother experienced a trauma once upon a time, a trauma that led to an inhibited and blocked Solar plexus chakra (underactivity). Her daughter, i.e. your mother grows up in this relationship with her mother and chooses on an unconscious level to compensate for this - she thereby creates an overactivity in her own Solar plexus chakra. She does this for two reasons! One is to create balance the energy and the other is because she is an empath and wants to relieve and help her mother. If a mother has underactivity in her Solar plexus chakra, the child is very likely to take over and develop a similar imbalance in her own Solar plexus chakra or develop the opposite, an overactivity. What determines which it will be is very much about the child's own sensitivity and empathic ability. It is common for children with high sensitivity/strong empathy to choose to relieve their mother's grief.

Another example is if your mother experienced trauma and created a blockage (underactivity) in her Heart Chakra. Her heart is filled with unprocessed grief and is somewhat closed. You feel like a child about this and start at an early age to give of your own energy and love to relieve her - compensate. An overactivity is created in your heart where you give and give and give. This can then follow as a pattern in future relationships where you choose a partner with a closed heart, where you go in and give and give.

We can also create an overactive chakra by overcompensating for something in ourselves, something we never got as a child. If you were never allowed to express your opinion as a child, you learned to be quiet and keep things to yourself. As an adult, you then begin to overcompensate for this – you choose to express your opinions in all contexts, have difficulty listening and may talk over other people.

An overactivity can also occur when we go in and heal a chakra that has been underactive. This is created because the chakra needs to be balanced and there in the transition, we can end up unbalanced in the other direction. This is common in our spiritual ascension and when we meet our Twin Flame /a strong soul connection. Many people who meet their Twin Flame find that they were previously very withdrawn and quiet, until they meet their Twin Flame. Then they can experience the opposite, that they start to take up a lot of space, have a strong need to be heard and make their voice heard - almost so that it becomes exaggerated in that direction. It is a common phenomenon when we are going to heal a chakra.

There will be a slight imbalance in the other direction before calm and balance is created in the chakra.

Our Seven Major Chakras

We will now take you on a journey through our seven major energy centers, our Chakras. All the chakras belong together and together form a whole and a prerequisite for our entire body to function optimally. Major imbalances in one chakra can affect other chakras. We have noticed that a lot of overactivity in one chakra can create underactivity in nearby chakras. So, if, for example, you have overactivity in your heart, there can be an underactivity in the Solar plexus chakra. It can also be the other way around, that you have overactivity in your Solar plexus chakra and, based on that, underactivity in the heart.

Another good example of what was mentioned above is the classic empath and the narcissist. There, the empath has an overactive Heart chakra and an underactive Solar plexus chakra, while the narcissist has the opposite – an overactive Solar plexus chakra and underactivity in the heart. These patterns lead the empath to give too much of their heart but too little in their power. The narcissist, on the other hand, is too much in his unbalanced power and too little in his heart.

Each chakra has a different function and is connected to different parts of our body. In order to gain access to energy and power and to be able to heal and create, we need to strive for as great a balance as possible in our chakras.

Below follows a presentation of each chakra where we also address how blockages affect us in life.

The Root Chakra

The root chakra is our first chakra and thus our base. It stands for our physical security, survival, stability, and power. The root chakra is extremely important as it forms the very foundation for us in life. We need to have a reasonable balance in this chakra to experience stability and a basic security. The chakra is also connected to our grounding, that is, our contact with Mother Earth and also our physical body. When we are not grounded, we may have a feeling that we are "up in the blue" or that we have difficulty being in our body. If we have experienced trauma or if we have escaped a lot from our body and our emotions, we may have difficulty getting in touch with our grounding.

The Root Chakra is already formed and developed during the time in the mother's womb, as early as at conception. This causes the chakra to sense and react to the energy that our mother carries and sends out when we are in the womb. If our mother carries very unprocessed emotions, strong fears, or trauma, we as highly sensitive/empaths will start to pick up these emotions and that energy right then and there. The chakra is also very central during our first years of life because then we depend on safety and security. It is also during the first years that we have the opportunity to build up an inner security, stability, and a fundamental base within us. If it is predominantly anxious and stressful around us at the age of 0-10, the Root Chakra will take a lot of damage.

In addition to this, the Root Chakra is connected with family, kindred and belonging. Through the Root Chakra, we bring with us inheritance, genes, and unhealed traumas from our family line. Here

93

we may need to work with healing where we free ourselves from major imbalances.

A balanced Root Chakra: We carry an inner security in ourselves and are able to take on things in life. We know we can handle unpredictable events, knowing we always have ourselves to fall back on. Things may happen around us, but we stand firm in our energy. We are in touch with our inner self and our emotions, which makes us grounded. Balance in the chakra allows us to make constructive decisions and solve things around us.

Blocked Root Chakra - emotional impact: We feel anxious, stressed, and powerless. We may also have difficulty landing, perhaps move a lot, experience an inner restlessness, and have great difficulty being present in our physical body. We may find it difficult to ground ourselves and struggle with a lot of emotional difficulties. Because our security is so important and fundamental to us, profound blockages and imbalances here will affect large parts of our life.

Other common signs of chakra imbalance are burnout, despair, or depression.

Since the Root Chakra is connected with physical survival, we can also have blockages in the chakra from previous lives, especially if we experienced trauma that meant a threat to life. An example of that is if we didn't have food for the day and maybe starved to death. It can sit as a cellular memory in this life and lead us to overeat or to be fixated on material security.

Blocked Root Chakra - physical impact: Our basic organs and systems in the body, the nervous system, spine, connective tissue, rectum, legs, feet, skeleton and lower part of the intestinal system and the bloodstream.

The Sacral Chakra

The Sacral Chakra is our second chakra, and it is connected to our creativity, sexuality, intimacy, closeness to others, creation, desire, relationships, and our emotions. The Sacral Chakra is very central during growing up as we learn to build and create relationships, get to know our body, develop our creative ability, and learn to manage our own emotions.

In addition to that, the chakra is strongly connected with our inner child and everything to do with playfulness and spontaneity. If we are inhibited, silenced as children or if we have a strict upbringing, this chakra can be damaged or create major imbalances. Let's say we are creative and expressive as children but are forced to suppress ourselves due to strict or stressed parents, which in turn shuts down and blocks that energy within us. The energy becomes blocked, and we create a pattern where we hold back and limit our way of being and behaving. An example of what it can look like is that as adults we find it difficult to be playful and that we have a great seriousness within us emotionally. We have a hard time allowing ourselves to relax and just enjoy life.

A child needs their parents' help in understanding and managing their emotions because they can sometimes be overwhelming for the child. If our parents cannot meet us in our feelings because of their own strong fears or inabilities, the child does not learn to deal with these in a balanced way. They may suppress their feelings and start to shut down. This in turn then continues into adolescence and then follows as a pattern when it comes to emotional management.

The Sacral Chakra is connected to our sexuality and our sexual energy. Sexual energy is not only connected to physical sexuality but is also about our ability to connect with other people, to be intimate with another person and to create a bond. If we don't learn it as children, it can be difficult to have well-functioning intimate relationships as an adult. If, as children, we were exposed to any form of abuse, regardless of whether it is sexual or something else, the Sacral Chakra will take a lot of damage. Abuse always occurs in relation to another person, and this can damage the child's confidence and ability to create functional and close bonds with other people.

A balanced Sacral Chakra: We express our feelings and our creativity in different areas of life. We find it easy to create intimate and close relationships and do not get stuck in patterns of dependency/rejection. We are independent while being able to be close to other people. In addition to that, we have a spontaneity and playfulness within us. When the Sacral Chakra is in balance, we have a healthy relationship with ourselves and with what happens within us. We have a good relationship with our emotions and can handle what happens to us.

Blocked Sacral Chakra - emotional impact: We may have difficulty with closeness, intimacy, and sexuality. It can show itself in different forms of dysfunctional patterns, for example that we are dependent on other people, that we cannot be in a relationship or that we have great limitations in the sexual sphere. Restrictions mean both sexual withdrawal, fear of sexuality and also the opposite, that we have an overactive sexuality. As people, we can be inhibited, emotionally shut down or find it difficult to express our creativity and creative power. We can also experience the opposite here, that we feel excessively strong unbalanced emotions in everyday life such as a lot of anger or fear. The sacral chakra is also connected with feelings such as guilt and if we carry a lot of guilt and responsibility, the cause often lies precisely in this chakra.

The Sacral Chakra is also connected with our relationship to other things than relationships, for example food, sugar, exercise, play, games, etc. This means that an unbalanced chakra can express itself via addiction in all these areas. We recognize it as gambling addiction, food addiction or exercise addiction.

Blocked Sacral Chakra – physical impact: Kidneys, upper intestines, bladder, reproductive organs and genitals, appendix, colon, pancreas, hips, pelvis, impotence, and uterus.

The Solar plexus chakra

The Solar Plexus chakra is our third chakra and it stands for our will power, inner strength, personal power, integrity and personality. It is also connected with our self-esteem and self-confidence - what we ourselves think we can handle.

As with the previous chakras, much of this chakra is founded during childhood and well into adolescence. It is during adolescence that we become increasingly aware of who we are and our identity. We learn to set boundaries and make choices based on ourselves.

Here it is important that we have parents who support us in this process and that they help us build healthy boundaries towards the outside world.

Many old souls and empaths have problems with this chakra as they often learned growing up that the needs and wants of others come before their own. There can also be major problems with integrity, standing up for oneself and setting clear boundaries. Many empaths find it difficult to really step into their full power and often put themselves a bit in the background. Due to the fact that many also go into adaptation, they lose their own willpower and ability to move forward in a clear direction. Old souls are extra sensitive and receptive to what happens in their surroundings, which often makes them extra vulnerable in childhood. To a greater extent than other children, they tend to take on and absorb the stress and negative emotions of their surroundings.

The Solar Plexus chakra is connected with our self-image and how we see ourselves. If we, as children, are strongly criticized and questioned, it can lead to us creating a strong criticism within ourselves. It settles as an imbalance in the chakra, and we are excessively critical of ourselves as adults. Empaths are in principle always critical of themselves, while people with narcissistic traits direct their criticism outwards at other people. Both aspects are rooted in an imbalance in the Solar Plexus Chakra.

A balanced Solar Plexus chakra: When the chakra is balanced, we experience a sense of security and strength within ourselves. We know who we are and set healthy boundaries towards other people. We value ourselves highly and have a fundamental belief that we can handle things that happen, whether they are everyday things or more challenging things. We don't let other people decide what is right for us or how we should do things.

Blocked Solar Plexus Chakra – emotional impact: Imbalances here are often shown through difficulties with boundary setting, that we "run over" ourselves and put others first. It can also manifest itself in the form of low self-esteem, low self-confidence and that we do not see our own potential. We feel powerless and have difficulty finding our direction in life. In addition, we may experience that we do not know who we are, and this makes it difficult for us to make adequate and true decisions in life. If our chakra is overactive, it can be shown by the opposite, that we know everything, can do the best, "run over" others and have a great need for confirmation.

Blocked Solar Plexus Chakra – physical impact: Stomach, liver, gall bladder, spleen, small intestines, adrenal glands, stomach and back.

The Heart Chakra

The Heart Chakra is our fourth chakra and the chakra located in the center of the chakra system. It is thus the chakra that connects our three higher and our three lower chakras in the body with each other. The heart chakra stands for love, passion, trust, our inner truth, forgiveness and compassion for ourselves and other people. Much of our healing power and soul energy is in our heart and it is through the heart that we can feel if something is really true for us. It is our direct link to our inner self, our life mission, and our soul.

The heart is a very important chakra and the strongest energy center we have. It is not so strange because the heart is the organ that keeps us physically alive. The heart has an incredibly strong power and when we create and attract from the heart, it has much greater power than when we create only through our thoughts. If we have difficulty attracting what we want in life, it can sometimes be because we only want something in the mind and that the heart is not really involved. If we are in our heart and follow its truth, we create from our interior. Past lifetimes have often been about physical survival, relationships, and power. These aspects belong more to our three lower chakras, and it is these chakras that have been dominant for many millennia and still are in many parts of the world. Today many wake up in the collective and begin their spiritual journey, which means a way home to our heart and soul. We have previously lived in the age of the Ego and now we are entering the age of the Heart. This means that more and more we need to let go of our ego and let our hearts rule. To be able to do that, we need to work a lot with our 3 lower chakras and heal old blockages and traumas.

Our Heart Chakra is connected to our ability to create higher spiritual connections, such as the connection between Twin Flames and other deep soul relationships. The difference between these relationships and somewhat more traditional relationships is the strong energy connection. The relationship between Twin Flames and other strong soul relationships is built around a strong energetic mechanism, rather than based on physical or sexual attraction. When there are large blockages in the heart, it becomes difficult to experience this divine and powerful energy flowing and we need to do a lot of healing in our lower chakras as well as in the heart to feel and experience that energy connection. This applies not only to our relationship with other people but our relationship with the divine and everything around us.

Many of you reading this book are probably familiar with the concept of codependency. This concept is closely related to the heart, and it means that we give a lot of our power and energy to another person, without getting much in return. This often starts already in childhood, and it is common for old souls and empaths to start giving of themselves and of their energy at an early age. This means that the heart is drained of energy, and it quickly becomes unbalanced. This can also be shown by the fact that we take a lot of responsibility for other people's well-being and that we put all our focus on helping/maintaining their well-being. Usually at the expense of our own health.

A balanced Heart Chakra: We have a healthy relationship with ourselves, with other people and with life. We treat ourselves with deep respect and care and follow what feels true to ourselves. In addition to that, we show compassion to the outside world without draining ourselves of energy and power. We know what we want and follow our inner convictions. There is a trust in everything that happens and in ourselves.

Blocked Heart Chakra – emotional impact: Blockages here can mean that we don't let people in close, lack of trust in people and life. We may find it difficult to forgive both ourselves and other people and experience difficulties with compassion and empathy. A blocked heart can create a feeling of closure and it is difficult for us to get in touch with our inner self.

Imbalance in the other direction can mean that the heart is too open and that we take in everything and everyone around us. It means that we stay too long in dysfunctional relationships, find it difficult to leave and that we give too much to others without getting as much back ourselves. We can also be a bit gullible and have a hard time seeing when people cause us harm.

Blocked Heart Chakra – physical impact: The heart, lungs, arms, hands, shoulders, thoracic spine, thymus, diaphragm, and our vascular system.

The Throat Chakra

The Throat Chakra is our fifth chakra, and it represents our Divine expression and our ability to make our voice heard in life. The chakra is also connected with our inner truth, our creative expression and how we express and show our emotions. If we hold back the feelings we really feel or the words we really want to express, these words and feelings can become locked energy and blockages in our throat.

The Throat Chakra is also connected with our ability to make decisions and to move forward in life. Many of us have blockages and underactivity in this particular chakra due to many past lives where we were silenced and lived in fear based on prevailing norms in society. Above all, women have been silenced throughout the millennia and thus have not been allowed to make their voices heard. This is deep in our collective consciousness and when we need to express ourselves, this energy reminds us.

A balanced Throat Chakra: We express ourselves freely and in a balanced way. Our inner voice guides us, and we feel safe in expressing our feelings. We feel that other people listen to us because we listen to ourselves. A balanced chakra means that we know when to create space and when it's time to back off a little. Another thing that characterizes balance here is that we make decisions and move forward in life.

Blocked Throat Chakra – emotional impact: When the chakra is blocked, we can have difficulty making our voice heard and getting out what we have to say in different contexts. We can also experience that we have throat problems, a lump in the throat, stuttering, muffled speech, social phobia, difficulty expressing emotions and difficulty making decisions.

Imbalance in the other direction can show itself through an excessive need to talk to others, a need to constantly be heard and seen and that we have difficulty listening to others. It can also be shown through excessive emotional expression.

Blocked Throat Chakra – physical impact: Throat, neck, jaw, teeth, mouth, throat, ears, nose, and hypothalamus.

The Third Eye

The Third Eye is our sixth chakra, and it stands for our intuition, our inner vision, imagination and dreams. The chakra is strongly connected with our intuitive part and our ability to receive intuitive messages and guidance. If we have an imbalance here, we may have difficulty perceiving our inner guidance, difficulty understanding our intuition and it may feel as if we have a membrane or a wall between ourselves and our inner self. By working with the Third Eye, restoring balance, and clearing the energy, we can gain more access to our intuition.

It is common for lightworkers to have major blockages in this chakra, due to previous lives where we had connection to various forms of spiritual work. Spirituality has for many centuries been considered wrong and even punishable, in relation to the church and its beliefs. There are many examples of people who had previous lives where they worked with healing, something that led to terrible punishments and sometimes death. In many cases it has caused blocked energy and major blockages in the Third Eye. We can also have dark energy that affects the chakra and prevents us from getting in touch with our gifts and our intuition.

A balanced Third Eye: When the Third Eye is in balance, we can see clearly, both internally and externally. We are free from illusions and see the truth within and around us. We can see images within us, fantasize and we see what our path in life is. We also have the ability to dream and to create through these dreams and visions. In addition to this, we have more or less access to our medial abilities.

Blocked Third Eye – emotional impact: When the chakra is blocked, we can experience difficulty concentrating, difficulty seeing our inner self and our life path, illusions, poor contact with our intuition, fear of our inner self and of working spiritually. We can also experience feelings of confusion and not really knowing what is what within ourselves.

Imbalance in the other direction can manifest itself through nightmares, extremely chaotic visions and impressions, overactive intuition, and chaos. It can also express itself through extreme beliefs and an exaggerated approach regarding one's own perception. An extreme example of that is a cult leader who believes he has access to the only truth.

Blocked Third Eye - physical impact: Head, the parotid gland, the forehead, hormones, eyes, ears, and the pituitary gland.

The Crown Chakra

The Crown Chakra is our seventh chakra, and it represents our awareness, universal knowledge, the universal self, our connection with the Universe and everything. The Crown Chakra is connected with the highest energy and wisdom of the Universe. The energy in this chakra is high, subtle, and powerful. This means that we need to work with the Root Chakra and be grounded in order to really open up and be very much in this high energy. If we are in contact with this energy without being grounded, we can experience confusion or even mental problems. The more stability we have in our lower chakras, the more our energy can move freely and smoothly up through the rest of our body and our higher chakras.

The Crown Chakra is also connected with our thoughts, programming, and outlook - how we see things. There are many people in today's society who have overactivity in this chakra, which is because society is structured a lot around our intellect, our thoughts and logic. To be successful and cope in today's society, we need to use and be a lot in our heads and our thoughts.

This causes overload in the Crown Chakra. Our thoughts and logic are connected to our masculine energy, and it is still that energy that dominates in society and in the world. To create balance, we need to bring in more of the feminine energy that touches the heart, our emotions, and our intuition. If as children we experience a lot of trauma and stress, we can use a defense mechanism where we somehow leave the body and go more into the head. We then lose contact with the body and our emotions, which creates what we call dissociation. People with a traumatic upbringing are often more up in their thoughts and often have little contact with their inner emotional life.

A balanced Crown Chakra: As a rule, we carry healthy and constructive thoughts about ourselves and life. We use our thoughts in a favorable way to move forward but at the same time have contact with the rest of the body and our emotions. Our thoughts are reasonably balanced, and we don't get stuck in recurring loops or chaos. When the chakra is in balance, we take in information and energy from outside, but filter and sort out things that disturb or affect us negatively. We also do not hold on to old templates and beliefs that no longer benefit us.

Blocked Crown Chakra – emotional impact: When the Crown Chakra is blocked, we can experience feelings of depression, negative thoughts, recurring negative thought patterns, fear, withdrawal, isolation, and difficulty coping with the outside world. We can also feel disconnected from everything and experience confusion.

Imbalance in the other direction can lead to confusion, chaotic thoughts and even psychosis. We find it difficult to be in the body and our thoughts are spinning all the time, which often causes sleep problems and a great deal of internal stress.

Blocked Crown Chakra – physical impact: Skin, muscles, brain, and central nervous system.

What blocks and shuts down our Chakras?

The following Emotions or conditions can shut down and block our chakras if they are not processed and dealt with in a constructive way. This does not mean that these feelings are the only ones that create imbalance in our chakras, but they are valuable to be aware of.

Root Chakra → **Fear**

The Sacral Chakra → **Guilt**

Solar Plexus Chakra → **Shame**

The Heart Chakra → **Unprocessed Grief**

The Throat Chakra → **Lies**

The Third eye → **Illusions**

Crown Chakra → **Attachment**

Our Ascension Chakras

In the previous part we went through our seven major and most basic chakras. Many choose to only work with them, and we get a long way through in-depth work with our main chakras. In this part, we want to give you the opportunity to deepen your knowledge of the chakra system. We have selected five additional chakras that you can develop and work with on your spiritual journey. One of these chakras is located under our feet and the other four vibrate above our head, a bit above the crown chakra and upwards. The further we get in our spirituality, the more profound work we may need to do. If you notice that you work a lot with your main chakras but that there is still a stop in your energy flow, it may be good to look at how things are with the other chakras.

When it comes to descriptions of our chakras, our energy system, and all things etheric, it's important not to get too rigid about each description. The descriptions aim to gain a basic understanding of how each chakra works and how we can access healing and its unique energy. In our physical world, things work via time and space in a linear fashion. In the etheric, things and processes happen in parallel, which means that we can switch back and forth in our development and in our healing. Feel free to use this understanding about your chakras and supplement with your own.

We call the 5 chakras we discuss here the Ascension chakras, which means that they are largely activated when we begin our spiritual awakening. It mainly applies to the four chakras above us which are all connected to our higher self, the galactic and also higher universal energies. By working with our ascension chakras, we can continue to expand and raise our consciousness and merge with the higher universal love energy that exists around us. The more we work on ourselves, heal our inner self, and let go of our ego, the more we move up in our chakras.

Generally speaking, our higher chakras are linked to our higher guides, other dimensions, the galaxy, and extraordinary gifts such as telepathy. They are also connected with our soul plane, past lives and our Akashic record. In the same way that it is important to work upwards with the chakras that we have in the body, the same principle applies here. We cannot skip working on our inner self and expect to reach amazing heights. We need to clear, heal, and follow our soul's life path to truly connect with our higher chakras. Look at how you can heal your inner self and follow what your heart longs for, but don't stress. Real development cannot be forced, and everything happens when you are ready.

Many of us will mainly work a lot with chakra 0 and chakra 8, as the two are connected to our foundation and our higher guidance and our connection with guides/our higher self. By working with and exploring these two chakras, you can go a long way and gain access to new understanding and power on your journey.

For you who are lightworkers and starseeds, these ascension chakras are important, and it is highly likely that you already have or will open and activate them in this lifetime. This is because it is part of your journey to be able to spread light to other people and the planet as a whole. You then need to have access to and use these chakras and their energetic qualities to fully step into your life task here on earth.

Chakra 0 – Earth Star Chakra

Our Earth Sar Chakra is located below the Root Chakra, directly under our feet. This means that the chakra is below us in contrast to the Root Chakra, which is located at the bottom at the end of the spine. The chakra is an extension of the Root Chakra, and we can see it as an extra root or "super root". Our Earth star chakra helps us reconnect with Mother Earth and her powerful healing energy on a deep level. The chakra is a link to our DNA and is thus also connected with our relatives and ancestors. Therefore, it is powerful to work with that chakra if we want to work on healing trauma from our lineage or restoring our DNA.

It is also valuable and helpful to focus on and work with this chakra if you have difficulties with your grounding and with insecurity. By focusing on this energy center, you amplify your power and create a solid foundation within yourself. Our Earth Star Chakra is strongly linked with the natural energies of the earth and one way to strengthen the chakra is to spend time in nature and in your own energy.

The chakra symbolizes our inner power of manifestation and when it is in balance, we gain access to enormous power that helps us in life. The chakra is also connected with all forms of life and already existed before we humans came to earth. This means that all animals and plants around us also have this chakra. Simplified, we can say that it is the chakra from which all living things derive their original power. In addition to what was mentioned, we also strengthen this chakra when we see ourselves and all living things around us as equal when it comes to value.

Chakra 8 – Soul Star Chakra

Our Soul star chakra is located above our head, approximately 10 centimeters above the crown chakra. The chakra is the portal between our physical body and our soul. By connecting or tuning into this energy center we access information from other dimensions, galaxies and also information from our Akashic records. The Soul Star Chakra helps us connect with higher light guides and with our place of origin, if we are starseeds. Think of this amazing chakra as a pathway or quick link between this, past and parallel lives. By working with the chakra, you can retrieve a wealth of information that is stored in your soul and in your etheric field. The chakra is like a bank where information is stored about your soul. This chakra is extremely important for you who are lightworkers and starseeds because the chakra is a prerequisite for being able to really connect and go fully into your soul energy. As a Starseed, you are used to living through and in these higher chakras at your home location, which makes it difficult for you to manage the lower chakras located in the body. Many starseeds get a shock when they come down into these more "low vibration" chakras and energies here on Earth.

The Soul Star Chakra is activated during life, for some early and for others later - depending on when we start our spiritual ascent and our inner journey. What we can do to activate this chakra is to work with our lower chakras, work with self-love, cleanse and heal our body. The probability that you have already activated the chakra is high and if not, it is positive to read this book and work with the exercises we cover.

Chakra 9 – The Spirit Chakra

Our Spirit Chakra is located above our Soul Star Chakra, and it guides us on our spiritual journey. The further you get on your spiritual journey the more you will open up and activate your higher chakras. This chakra requires us to let go of the ego and also of self-criticism and judgment. We need to open up to unconditional love, towards ourselves and others. We also need to see our own value and greatness in the form of a powerful creator, part of the Divine.

Many lightworkers and starseeds have great difficulty when it comes to seeing and feeling their own worth and this is largely due to the fact that many of them choose to go into codependency early on when they come down to Earth. They begin to attune to more low frequency and heavy energy and may then find it difficult to regain and re-enter their divine power. But this is part of the journey, and it happens when the person is ready.

Chakra 10 – The Galactic Chakra

Our Galactic Chakra represents divine creation of various forms – sharing one's gift to the outside world. When we have this chakra open, we gain access to higher levels of consciousness within ourselves, and we partake of information and creation from the Universe. The chakra is also about spreading one's light and letting divine light shine through us and out into the world. When we decide to step into the role of light worker and make a difference for humanity, this chakra is activated and we gain access to higher information, healing, and creative energies. This usually happens in connection with our spiritual awakening and when we consciously set a clear and deep intention to help.

To get here, you need to be willing to dare to go through all the pain and resistance you feel in order to move forward. This chakra is opened and balanced when you fully choose your own life path, the path of your soul that you will walk in this life. This is very challenging and difficult for many lightworkers because there can be an idea that it should feel easy and positive to evolve. But it takes a lot of courage and determination to face one's inner darkness and transform it into light. It's like cutting a diamond - it takes a lot of grinding before the diamond shines brightly.

Chakra 11 – Universal Chakra

Our Universal Chakra unites us with the Universe and the higher light guides on an energetic level. To get here we need to see ourselves as a thoroughly divine energetic being, filled with light and power. The ego is not included here, but our intentions and actions are guided by higher intentions and through our higher self.

The chakra is also linked with extraordinary abilities such as telepathy, contact with other galaxies and astral travel. It usually takes many lifetimes before we achieve balance and come into contact with this state. An example of a person who we can assume was on this plane a lot was Jesus when he was alive. He lived fully in his life mission, helped other people and was free from judgment. Furthermore, he had a strong connection and contact with God or the source, the purest and highest energy.

How can we heal our Chakras?

In the previous part we have gone through our 12 chakras and now it is time to look at how we can work on healing and balancing them. The main focus is on our seven main chakras, as they are central to begin with. When you learn to work with them, you can also work in the same way with your other chakras.

There are many ways to work when it comes to our chakras and our way differs a lot from the ways that are often found in many other traditions. Examples of different ways that exist are working with yoga, various physical exercises, colors, meditations, and crystals. There is absolutely nothing wrong with these methods and they work well for many people. It is also possible to combine those methods with what we cover in this book. We have noticed in our own internal work as well as in the work with clients, that these methods are not always quite enough. Many of the people we meet are star seeds and old souls, which means that they have a lot of big challenges with them, both from childhood and from previous lives. This means that the problems and blockages that exist are often complex and very deep.

A big challenge for old souls when it comes to the society we live in today, is that we are constantly being fed information about how to take care of ourselves. We see newspaper headlines and various programs where experts in various fields highlight how we should eat, what we need to keep our bodies in shape and what kind of relationship we should be in. To really move forward and find inner balance in life, we need to realize that there is only ONE expert for us and that is ourselves. You need to become your own expert and understand what your body and soul need. We are so used to listening to what others say that we no longer know what is good for us. Even as children, we learn in school what is important, right, good, wrong, and how we should be in order to succeed in life. But to heal ourselves and reconnect with our soul, we need to learn to understand ourselves so well that we know what our body is trying to tell us.

If you play with the idea that you are a soul that has lived many lives before, probably upwards of a hundred maybe thousands of lives. Based on everything you've been through - all the experiences, all the tragedies, all the successes, all the perspectives and insights -

would someone else from the outside know better about you than yourself? That doesn't mean you have to do everything on your own. It can be valuable and helpful, perhaps even crucial, to sometimes take outside help to move forward. Sometimes we don't see what's going on because it's so close. We can take help from others we trust, but in the end, we have ourselves to rely on. When we do that, we take back the power within ourselves and we raise our self-worth, because we actually believe in ourselves and what we can do. When it comes to our chakras, we work with Energy Healing or Energy Work. This means that we help to move energy – we make the energy move. That's what energy work and healing is all about, helping to get energy going that has been blocked and to create balance where the energy is flowing too much.

In the first chapter of the book, we explained how blockages are created in our energy system. The energy is stopped up and encapsulated, which in turn creates stagnation and various symptoms - because the energy is no longer reaching the body. So, what we need to do to get the energy flow going is simply to work with the energy. It's not always easy, but it doesn't have to be that hard either. We often have an idea that healing is something complicated and that only some people can do it. You always have the ability to heal everything within you and many times it can be enough to become aware of something in the body for the energy to start moving. The difficult thing is not always to find blockages, but to dare to face what we encapsulated, the pain and the memories that can come up in connection with the healing.

In this chapter, we have compiled knowledge, materials, and exercises that we consider helpful and that we ourselves use a lot in our daily work with ourselves, clients and in our courses. We strongly believe in the importance of cleansing, cleansing, and cleansing. To constantly work through new layers in different chakras. The more we heal and clear, the more we access underlying things and new layers of blockages. It may sound tough but the more you work at it and get into it the more routine it becomes. We go through our chakras and cleanse our energy system every day, which for us is necessary in our work. It's a bit like keeping the house clean - better to tidy up a little every day than to collect everything in a pile.

When it comes to spiritual development, there is no shortcut, we need to take courage and dive deep. We need to get through the resistance and blockages we encounter. The reward will be worth all the work, as we let go of karma and blockages we have carried for many years or lifetimes. In addition, healing gives us access to our spiritual gifts and helps embody more light, that is, more of our soul. On top of that and perhaps best of all – we get more of our amazing energy back!

The process of Healing through the Chakras

You have probably heard of Maslow's hierarchy of needs in psychology. If not, it is the theory of a staircase that symbolizes our human needs. At the bottom of the stairs are our basic needs such as safety, food, and sleep. The further up the ladder we go, the more these needs shift to personal development and self-realization. The important thing about the stairs is that we need to start at the bottom and then work our way up in our development. We cannot work on self-realization if we live under threat or do not have food for the day. The same is true with our chakras – we need to start at the bottom and then work our way up. We need to do the grunt work first before we can tap into our amazing gifts and our full potential. To fully develop our higher chakras, we first need to create balance and healing in the lower ones. It is incredibly important and a crucial key in our healing journey.

Let's say you have major blockages in your Root Chakra, blockages that create a fundamental insecurity and fear in you. As long as you have it, you cannot fully enter into your life force nor fully open up to the divine. Your soul will not allow that and since it is your soul that is leading you forward, it wants to make sure that you are ready and able to handle these big steps forward.

If we look at your Solar Plexus Chakra, it's about finding who you are, setting boundaries, being yourself and being in your power. Without balance in these parts, it becomes basically impossible to enter into and carry out your life task and what you came here to do. You need to know who you are, stand up for yourself and reclaim your unique power to then create and manifest this externally. This is incredibly important for you who are lightworkers and starseeds. You have great things to accomplish here on earth. A lot to accomplish often means a lot of inner work.

In order for you to realize and live through your soul, you need to face the darkness and the heaviness that lies in the way. As long as your body is full of locked energy and blockages, there is no room for high energy to enter.

In the times we live in, it is extremely important to dare to go inward, to dare to face oneself. If you want to know what is really standing in the way of you and your soul - look at the pain you carry and avoid. Facing the darkness and pain is the path to your freedom and to your light. We've said it before and we'll say it again; the more you dare to face your inner self, the more development takes place! Darkness is nothing but stagnant energy, unprocessed emotions, low frequency energy and unconsciousness. As long as it is in our subconscious it can do great harm, when we lift it up it is transformed into light and awareness.

As for the exercises we cover, you can either use your intuition and feel directly or use pendulum (Kinesiology works too). We recommend using a pendulum if you feel unsure about feeling in freely. The pendulum is an extension of your intuition and through it you receive answers from your higher self and your guides.

Below is a selection of exercises you can use to heal and balance your chakras.

Awareness

When it comes to all forms of spiritual work and energy work, awareness is important - becoming aware of things. Just by becoming aware of something within you, you have healed around 50 percent of the problem. The reason for that is that most of what we carry is on an unconscious level. Becoming aware helps start a healing process on a deeper level.

So, imagine that you discover that there is locked energy/a blockage in your Root Chakra. This blockage makes you feel insecure and afraid in daily life. By bringing it out, that particular blockage begins to release, and the energy begins to move in the chakra. Many times, we think we need to do a lot to heal, but healing is more about becoming aware and allowing the healing to happen. So, bringing up blocks and then letting go and trusting that we are healing is an important part.

This can be challenging many times as we would like to know, get confirmation, do something purely practical or understand things purely intellectually. It is especially difficult for those of you who have a tendency to be in your head a lot. But just know that the healing starts as soon as we lift things up to the surface and dare to look at them. Remember that healing takes place even if you don't always feel it physically. We can work with a chakra and clear blockages without feeling so much in the moment. Sometimes it comes afterwards. Trust that all the healing and energy work you do create a difference in your inner being - EVERYTHING! Every intention, every clearing, and every time you put your full focus on something changes the energy within you. Sometimes it can feel like we're standing still or that nothing is happening, but that's because we have many layers and new things are emerging to heal.

Learn the language of your Chakras

We highly recommend that you take time to get to know your chakras, and their specific energies. In order for your physical body to feel good, you need to know what suits it, how long you need to sleep, what kind of activity it feels good from, food, etc. The same is true with your chakras. Spend time really understanding each chakra. Observe how you function in life and in different contexts.

Ask yourself the following questions about your childhood:

♡ Were there major fears/insecurities/trauma in childhood?

♡ Could I express myself freely?

♡ Was there room to be myself?

♡ How was the view of sexuality? Was there abuse?

♡ Was it okay to show emotions?

♡ Were there certain feelings that were not okay to feel?

♡ Did I get help to deal with my inner self when it was tough?

♡ Did either of my parents have a lot of their own fears/unprocessed trauma?

♡ Did I take care of any parent excessively if only emotionally?

♡ Was there closeness, love, and hugs?

The above questions are examples of areas that often create greater blockages within us connected with our chakras. Feel free to look at each question and investigate whether patterns have been created based on what you carry with you today. Children who assume excessive responsibility for one or both parents at an early age tend to continue that pattern into adulthood. This means that we enter into what is familiar and familiar to us. It could be shown by us looking for a relationship where the other has narcissistic traits and where we do everything to take care of and make things good for that person.

Ask your Guide Team for help
In our work, we take a lot of help from higher light guides when we work with our chakras. Our higher light guides have a very high healing energy, and they see our life path from above, from a higher perspective. At any time, you can ask your higher self, a guide or

several guides for help to clear your chakras, heal blockages, transform heavy emotions and to bring healing to a certain area. When you ask them for help, they come to you. Be sure of that, even if you don't always see or feel them. You don't need to have any special formula or express yourself in the right way, all you need to do is the following:

- Ask for help and express what you want help with.
- Allow help to come through trust! By having trust, you open up for the flow and healing to come through.
- Be open to help coming in the form it is meant to. Let go of notions that it should happen in a certain way.
- Say Thank you for the help!

It might sound like this:

"I ask Archangel Michael for help to let go of old things that hold me back and to clear that blockage in the Heart Chakra. Help me to heal on a cellular level and on all other levels. I am ready to let go of what limits me! I trust that I will get the help I need, thank you!"

Exercise 1: Healing chart

An effective way to work with our chakras is through charts. It can help you clearly see which chakra to work with and where healing is needed. The image on the next page shows a chart of your seven main chakras. You can make a similar map, either in the computer or just draw by hand. It doesn't have to be pretty, but the main thing is that it's clear. We recommend that you either feel freely which chakra you are attracted to or use a pendulum. Then just place the pendulum at the bottom of the black dot and ask questions. The pendulum will then show which chakra applies. For example, you can ask questions such as:

- Which chakra do I need to work on right now?
- Which of these chakras is most out of balance based on my upbringing?
- Is there raw trauma in any chakra, if so, which?
- Which chakra affects my intimate relationships the most right now?

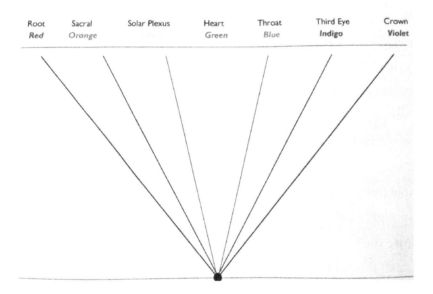

Root	Sacral	Solar Plexus	Heart	Throat	Third Eye	Crown
Red	Orange		Green	Blue	Indigo	Violet

You can also ask free questions in addition to the chart itself. Let's say you discover that there is a blockage in the Heart Chakra. Ask more questions with the pendulum:

- Do I have chakra underactivity? (for example No)
- Do I have overactivity? (Yes)
- Did the blockage occur in the chakra in this life? (Yes)
- Was it when I was a child? (Yes)
- What feeling is associated with the blockage? Anger? (No) Grief? (Yes) etc.

This method may feel a little complicated at first, but it is a matter of habit. It is a very effective way of finding blockages that we ourselves are not aware of and that we need to work on. Often, we find it difficult to find things within ourselves and it is not always the case that we sense certain blockages purely emotionally. Nevertheless, the energy is there and affects us. You can work on this exercise every day, from time to time or when you feel it is needed. New things will come up every time you are ready to work and remember, just by becoming aware you have done half the job. When you find out what type of blockage you have or just know that there is a blockage, you can ask more follow-up questions if you want to investigate the whole thing a little more, such as in the example above. Then ask your higher self, a guide, or several guides for help to heal and release the blockage within you. If you are unsure which guide to ask, ask that the guides who can help you best assist you.

Exercise 2: Directed Energy Healing

In this exercise, it's about finding a blockage through a feeling you experience, that is, you capture a feeling and derive it to a chakra in the body. When we experience strong emotions such as anger, sadness, guilt, shame, pain, fear, panic, anxiety or discomfort, these emotions are in principle always connected to a chakra. They are often connected with our three lower chakras, due to the fact that our lower chakras relate more to our raw and primitive emotions and lower vibrational emotions. It is low frequency energy that we feel, in the form of emotions. Of course, we can also experience emotions that are associated with our other chakras.

By stopping up when we feel a certain feeling and finding where in the body it is, we can find which chakra the blockage is in. When we find which chakra the blockage is in, we can begin to dissolve and release the locked energy that limits us. This doesn't have to be difficult, and anyone can work with this.

There is one thing that is important to remember and that is that our ego and inner resistance can make themselves known here. If you feel resistance or if strong fear comes up before the exercise or during the exercise, just pay attention to what you experience without acting on it - that is, experience and be in the resistance and observe it until it subsides. Trust it to go away!

So, to the exercise itself:

- Let's say you feel an emotion, for example anger. It can be a weak or strong feeling. Go inside and feel the feeling fully, stay in the rage! If it works, welcome the feeling.
- This may take some practice if you are not used to it, but the more you learn to be in your emotions the easier you can heal and heal yourself.
- Find where in the body the feeling is. In this case, the feeling may be in the upper part of the stomach, which is the Solar

Plexus Chakra. This means that there is a blockage in this chakra. The energy does not flow as it should.

- So, once you have identified in which chakra the blockage is, put your full focus there. Feel the feeling! It may happen that the feeling becomes stronger and that is completely okay. Be in the feeling until it starts to subside. It may take a few seconds or longer.

- It may even be that the feeling is replaced over time and turns into sadness, guilt, or something else. Let it happen! Just feel what comes without judging whether it is right or wrong.

- When the feeling subsides and you feel yourself starting to find a neutrality, it's done for now. The blockage begins to release and the energy moves.

- What happens here is that you put your focus on the place where the energy is locked and when we focus on energy, it starts to move. Were your focus goes – energy flows.

- Sometimes thoughts may appear during the time that are connected to this or some memory. Just observe it and allow it to come and go. You don't need to do any analysis or understand everything. Just let your body and energy do the work!

- If you want, you can also ask your higher self or the guides to step in with healing, to balance the chakra and clear out things that shouldn't be there.

So, in short:

→Feel the feeling

→Find where in the body it is

→Identify the chakra

→Focus and feel

→The energy begins to flow

→The blockage is released

If you learn to work in this way, you will be able to do it at any time, even out on the town if necessary. You eventually learn quickly to pick up and identify different emotions and states. Since we have many different layers of blockages in the body, these feelings can come back at a later time and then we can do the same process again. Eventually we have released most of what is attached to it. Be aware that it can take time and healing can be likened to a spiral. Sometimes we think that nothing is happening or that we have failed because the same feeling repeats itself, but this is not the case. Every time you consciously work with something within you, healing takes place. But because we are complex and carry layers of blockages from different ages and lifetimes, we may have to face the same emotions over and over again. It may also be that we need to change something in practice. So, if you have been working a lot with a chakra and notice that it is slow, see if there is something you can do or change in practice. Maybe you need to stand up for yourself and set more clear boundaries? Maybe you give away too much of your power and energy to your mother when you see each other?

Exercise 3: Finding a Blockage

You can do the following exercise if you want to find and work with blockages in your chakras but do not experience any special feelings at the moment. This method is also suitable if you have difficulty getting in touch with your feelings or your inner self. Then you can instead sense, ask or commute whether there is any blockage in a particular chakra. Here is a good opportunity to use the pendulum, if you don't want to feel in completely freely with intuition. If you find that there is a blockage in the Heart Chakra, you can then ask for help to dissolve the blockage and release the locked energy - trust that it will happen! It could look like this:

- Do I have a blockage in the Root Chakra? (You can of course take any chakra or several)
- If you get a yes to that, put your full focus on the Root Chakra. Just put your focus there, maybe some feeling, or thought will come or it's just still. It's okay either way. If feelings come, stay in the feeling - experience the feeling until it subsides.
- If you don't feel anything, you can ask your higher self or any guide of your choice to help you unblock and release the energy that is locked up. Trust that you will get help and you will ALWAYS get help! For example, use Archangel Michael here.
- The blockage begins to dissolve, and feelings associated with this may come up for a while afterwards or even a few days afterwards. We don't always feel it, but feelings can come up once the blockage is released. So, pay attention to feelings that come up afterwards and allow them to flow and leave your body.

Don't get caught up in doing exactly the right way but play around a bit with the exercises - maybe you'll find elements of other things that you want to include. Your intention to let go and your trust that it will let go is crucial to your healing.

Exercise 4: Healing for a Theme

This exercise is great if you want to focus on a particular area such as a health condition or something else. Start by choosing a topic you want to work on. We take an example here with burnout. You can use intuition freely, use pendulum or a combination of both. A tip is to try to feel freely during this exercise. If it doesn't work or if it's slow, you can use the pendulum.

For the exercise itself:

1. Ask questions! Is there a block in terms of burnout? (Yes)
2. If yes, in which chakra or chakras is the blockage located? (pay attention to the body's reactions)
3. Start with the first chakra you received.
4. What is this blockage trying to tell you?
5. Let intuition flow and let go. Perhaps an event, a person, a year and, above all, one or more feelings appear.
6. If in doubt, ask if it is from this life or a past life!
   Keep looking until you have an image within you that feels reasonably clear.
7. Here, many may become uncertain and think that it is their imagination that comes in, but the line between here is often very fine. Trust that what comes to you has meaning.

8. When you feel ready, feel free to ask your higher self or higher guides for help in healing the burnout and accessing the originating event. The originating event is the time when the block was created.

9. You can do the same thing with several different areas. As soon as you open up in this way, you will access the energy and emotions that have been locked in connection with that state.

Exercise 5: Over - or Underactivity

Here are two simple exercises you can do if you have an underactive or an overactive chakra. If you are not sure how things are with your chakras, you can ask and get help with a pendulum. You can also take help of the descriptions found around each chakra in the previous part, to see if you recognize yourself in something there. When it comes to underactivity and overactivity, we may need to work both with energy healing and changing different patterns in our appearance. If there is underactivity, we want to start the energy flow in the chakra, and if there is overactivity, we want to reduce the flow and create a calm. In this case, we take the Throat Chakra as an example.

Underactivity

Put your full focus on the Throat Chakra for a few minutes or as long as you like and ask your higher self or higher guides to replenish energy in the chakra and to balance it until the energy flows more freely. Ask for help to heal and transform heavy energy and to heal cellular memories from past lives that affect the chakra.

Overactivity

Put your full focus on the Throat Chakra for a few minutes or as long as you like while asking your higher self or the guides to reduce the energy in the chakra and restore it to its normal state and to its optimal energy flow. Also ask for help to repair the chakra and to clear negative energy that is affecting.

Powerful tips for your 7 Chakras

In addition to the above exercises, it is positive if you can change patterns and behaviors on the outside, to create a powerful change. So, if you think or know you have throat underactivity, do what you can to get the flow going. Sing, express yourself, express your feelings, make clear decisions, and dare to move forward in life. If, on the other hand, you have an overactivity in the chakra, it is positive if you can practice listening to yourself and perhaps also others, express yourself in a more balanced way and work on relaxation. In the text below, there are further tips on how you can have balance in each chakra.

The Root Chakra

To create balance in your Root Chakra, it is important that you work with your inner security. Look at what creates anxiety and fear within you. Do things, exercises and activities that create a calm and that help ground your energy. Something that often helps us to become grounded and calm is to be in nature from time to time. So, feel free to visit nature and take time where you are just with yourself. When you are with yourself in a calm environment, it becomes easier for you to feel yourself and your own energy. The more security you create in yourself, the easier other challenges in life become, both internally and externally. Any kind of physical activity is good for this chakra, as long as it is done in a balanced way. Exercise, run, go for a walk. Do things where you get in touch with your body.

The Sacral Chakra

To have a Sacral Chakra in balance, it is valuable for you to create and be creative. Do things that awaken your playfulness and desire. Find activities and contexts where these feelings are brought to life. Dancing, playing and various forms of physical activity where you can act freely open up the energy in this chakra. If you find it difficult to be with other people, put on music at home when you are alone and dance away. If it's uncomfortable, it's absolutely the right way to go. A lot of locked energy in the Sacral Chakra is about us holding back ourselves and our energy. All forms of creation and spontaneity help the chakra to become more balanced. Express your feelings and allow yourself to enjoy life. Allow yourself to feel all the emotions, joy, lust, sexuality, pleasure, and other things that are part of you. Let go of your self-criticism and meet your inner child. Listen to what it has to say to you.

The Solar Plexus Chakra

Be proud of yourself and who you are. Look at everything you've been through in life and find the pride within. Pride is celebrating yourself and what you are. Affirm yourself and set your own worth high. You are the most important person in your life - you are the main character in your movie. When you respect yourself and your feelings, other people do the same. When you set clear and real boundaries based on what feels good to you, people around you will meet you with respect. Find what is yours and what is you, rather than attributes others have attributed to you. Allow yourself to be yourself, just as you are. Maybe you are introverted, extroverted, forward or more withdrawn. No matter how you are, allow yourself to be who you are. Allow yourself to step back when you feel like it, but also allow yourself to be powerful when it's time.

The Heart Chakra

Whatever has been, forgive yourself. Whatever you have felt, allow yourself to forgive yourself. Give yourself love, compassion and forgiveness. Do not hold on to old sorrow and pain but set yourself free by forgiving what has been. You have always done the best you could, in every given moment. Dare to open up and receive love, even if it means you might get hurt. Give to others but give even more to yourself. When you give love to yourself, you fill your heart, which creates even more to give to others. Don't give your power away to others, stand in your power and open up to love in all its forms. Allow yourself to let go of old pain and sorrow. You don't have to carry it anymore.

The Throat Chakra

Express yourself in life and show who you are. Don't hold yourself back but show with pride what is important to you. You don't have to hide who you are. The world needs you and your amazing energy. Dare to face fears that are within you, fears that have been created over hundreds of years. Don't be someone you're not, but don't hold back what you are either. When you express yourself and your truth, you show the way to others. You guide others by being yourself in life. Sing, laugh and use your voice in a way that brings you joy. It helps you dissolve stagnant energy and chakra blockages. Express your emotions such as crying, laughing, anger or sadness. Don't hold back but transform what you carry by expressing it in some form.

The Third Eye

Look at what are your dreams, goals, and visions. Many in society live based on ideas and beliefs created by society and its prevailing norms. Dare to see things your way and find your dreams and goals in life. Don't let the environment or anyone else limit you when it comes to what you know or can do. Practice sensing what feels good to you, free from other people's expectations and demands. Dare to do things outside the box, even if it means that others don't agree or go the exact same way as you. Dare to dream and have confidence that what you dream about will come true.

The Crown Chakra

This chakra gains balance when you let go of control of how things must or should be. Let go of ideas and beliefs that no longer benefit you and that hold you back. Don't hold on to old things that weigh you down and allow yourself to let go of old relationships and people who don't help you or add anything to your life. Open up to new ways of looking at things and create new templates and approaches in society. The world does not need more people who think alike, but people who think new - who create and drive themselves and others forward.

Do relaxation exercises and try to let go of the focus on your thoughts, preferably for a little while a day. Our thoughts are often connected with our limitations, fears, and ingrained patterns. By allowing your thoughts to rest and go more into your body, you help calm and balance the chakra.

Chapter 9

DARK AND NEGATIVE ENERGY

As we mentioned earlier, all the blockages we have chosen to address in this book are important and in some cases even crucial to understanding oneself deeply and undergoing deep healing. It is important to know when it comes to energy work that nothing is set in stone and that everything can be interpreted in different ways. The important thing is not to be right or wrong about something but to access what actually limits you in your life, so that you can create and live more through your soul and its unique energy.

Energy blockages are, as said, some type of blocking, locked energy that sits somewhere in our energy system - from this or a previous life. It is energy that we need to release and set in motion and thereby release the blockage.

Dark energy

The universe consists of both light and darkness in the same way that these contrasts also exist in our existence. When we look around the world, we will see contrasts of everything. We see people who act more out of their ego, even darkness and people who act out of pure love. It is part of being here on earth as a human being and it is meant to be, until we are ready to raise the collective consciousness and thus the vibration of the planet. There are planets and soul groups that exist only in the light while other places are more dominated by lower energy and darkness.

What then is the difference between light and darkness? It is a complex question but in a simplified way we can say that darkness is energy that vibrates at a very low frequency while light is energy that vibrates at a very high frequency. Examples of this are love and fear. Love has a pure high frequency and when we act based on love, we raise our energy frequency. Fear has a low frequency and when we make many choices based on fear we lower our energy frequency. The further up we go on this scale the brighter it gets and the lower we go down the more darkness.

Dark energies are thus low-frequency energies that affect us in different ways. It can be energy from people around us who live in a very low frequency, and it can also be energy from souls we have around us on an astral level. Going even further, there can be very dark energy, connected with soul groups and other astral beings.

An example of how negative energies can be created in our existence is if a person directs very strong negative thoughts and negative intentions towards us. The energy that is directed at us then becomes very low and we can sense and be affected by this, especially if we are emotionally bound or connected with the person. An example of how negative energies can be created from past lives is if we have been exposed to very dark and heavy things in one life. Maybe we worked with spirituality and were reported before the church whereupon the church punished us and pronounced a curse on us. This energy can then accompany us from life to life and every time we try to get started with our spiritual work, we are met by a "wall", that is, this negative energy that comes up.

We are humans living on Earth but as we are multidimensional beings we are constantly interacting with other souls and energies in other dimensions. We feel energies and emotions from people around us, from places and we can also pick this up from other souls in our soul group - this because we are all connected on a higher level. Souls in our soul group can affect us negatively through their presence if they carry a lot of fear and are left with heavy energies from previous lifetimes.

There are two times when we often get much lower or dark energies affecting us; one is when we ourselves live in very heavy frequencies, that is, we feel very bad and have poor contact with our inner self. The reason for that is that like attracts like and our heavy vibration emits and attracts similar energy. We can see this, for example, when we feel bad and feel that everything around us is going badly. We attract more of the same!

The second time is when we take big steps forward and enter our light, that is, when we raise our vibration and get closer to our inner self. We might start a company where we work with healing, and we feel that we are really moving forward. Suddenly everything feels heavy, and that light turns into a sluggish mud that we struggle through. This is because when we go more into our light, our light can be perceived as a threat by other energies. Think of all the movies you've seen, both as a child and as an adult. The better things go for the main character, the more resistance there usually comes from the enemy or from evil. If the main character just sits at home on the couch and relaxes, there will hardly be any external resistance that makes things difficult.

In our physical existence, we may sometimes experience people around us trying to diminish us or hold us back, because they feel threatened by our light and success. In the same way, this happens on a soul level and other souls can affect us negatively without us being aware of it. Examples of historical figures who are believed to have experienced this are Jesus and Buddha, who we believe were both great healers but who encountered a lot of opposition and darkness from outside. Overall, negative, or dark energy is not directly dangerous, but it can limit and hinder us in many different ways. The more we step into our power, the harder it becomes for other people and energies to affect us. It may still be there, but we are safe and stable enough that we don't let it affect us like that.

Dark energy and resistance can also be part of our journey on Earth as Lightworkers. It can also be connected to our life task and what we are here to do. Without resistance, we do not get the opportunity to take the enormous steps forward and grow as it is meant to. That doesn't mean it should always be seen as something positive, but it is what it is. Our task will then be to relate to it, work with our fears and clear a lot of our energy.

In some cases, individuals are very visibly affected by dark energies, and this can create major problems, physically, emotionally and energetically. It may be because they took it upon themselves as a task in this life to transform and work with very heavy and dark energy. It can also mean that due to various reasons you have taken on a lot of heavy and dark energy that you need to free yourself from. It is important to know that we carry enormous power within us and that we can always transform what we need and what we have within and around us. Sometimes we may need a little support and help along the way.

In our own work, we have had to face an enormous amount of resistance and darkness, partly because of the work we work with, partly because of our origin as starseeds. Some starseeds and souls from specific soul groups have more contact with darkness than others, for slightly different reasons. We really want to emphasize the importance of getting into and understanding this work, especially if you know or notice that you are often pulled down by weight and resistance. The greater things we are here on earth to accomplish, the more darkness and opposition we are likely to encounter. There is sometimes a certain perception within the spiritual world that everything is just light and love and from a higher perspective this is true. Everything is created in universal love and will eventually return to that state. But as long as we live here on earth and want to progress within ourselves, we need to be well aware of lower aspects that affect us. Actually, it is no more strange than that we meet people around us here who disturb us or affect us negatively. Without the deep cleansing work we did for ourselves in our work, we would not have done what we do today. It has been crucial in many ways to get us where we are going in this life. There are more forms of darkness than we cover in the book, but we have chosen what we believe to be the most common.

Examples of different forms of dark energy that can affect us:

- Other people's negative intentions towards you.
- People in your environment with whom you have very heavy karma.
- Outer dark energy in the form of dark guides (there are both light & dark guides).
- Outer dark energy that is connected with, for example, the church/religion.

- Dark energy that works against light and development.
- Entities of various kinds.
- Energy we picked up from other souls/soul groups.
- Very heavy feelings and fears within us in the form of old trauma.
- Very dark energy in the form of reptilian energy, devil energy & curses.

How to clear Dark Energy

When it comes to any kind of work and clearing of dark energy, it is important that we learn more and more to discern our own energy. We need to know how our own basic energy feels in order to notice when we are receiving external or other people's energies. So, if you are unsure of your own energy, you can start observing it a little more during the day. Feel free to stop a few times a day and feel how it feels. Many times, we know when we are in our own energy even if we don't think about it. A common sign that we get a little more heavy or dark energies into our energy system is that we feel different, strange and that we don't really recognize ourselves. We can also experience strong fear and experience that things feel very sluggish. Dark energy can also manifest itself in the fact that we suddenly find it difficult to sense and receive higher guidance, although we are usually able to do so. Sometimes it is enough to clear away dark energy once, but it is more common that we may need to clear repeatedly. We almost need to see it as part of our daily work, to keep clean and clear our energy.

Archangel Michael is a fantastic guide to work with when we want to clear and free ourselves from old baggage and darkness in various forms. Often it is enough to work with Archangel Michael, but sometimes we recommend that you use several guides, especially if you notice that it does not really help and if there is a lot of darkness. Guides besides Michael that are good to take help of are The Arcturians. When we work with guides and angels, we never have to think about whether it is okay or whether they are available, but as soon as you set an intention to work with them, they are with you.

Exercise to Clear

Start by asking or feeling if there is any negative or dark energy affecting you right now, either just straight up and down or with the help of the pendulum. If you use a pendulum, be sure to clean the pendulum as clean as possible, as this will give you cleaner responses.

For example, you can ask:

- Is there some dark energy affecting me right now? (Yes)
- Can it be cleared? (Yes)
- Ask for cleansing: I ask Archangel Michael to cleanse all forms of darkness in my energy system. Clear all negative, dark, and heavy energy that is not mine and that is holding me back. Thanks!
- Is the energy gone? (Yes)

Often it is enough to do it that way and remember that the important thing is not to say the right words, but to have a clear intention with what you want to do - in this case, clear energy. You may need to cleanse several times and sometimes a little every day.

You will eventually learn to discern when it is time to go in and clear. Sometimes you may need to work more with the energy to get it out. You may need to find out where it is, for example in the aura, some chakra, in the entire energy system, etc. You may also need to understand what the energy is about and perhaps make a change in your life. If you notice that the energy does not disappear, you can ask further:

- Is the energy in any chakra? (Yes)
- Root Chakra? (No)
- The Sacral Chakra? (Yes)
- Can it be cleared right now? (No)
- Do I need to do anything else? (Yes)
- Is it something practical? (Yes)
- Does it have to do with my family? (No)
- Is it related to a previous relationship? (Yes)
- Does he still affect me energetically? (Yes)
- Is this information enough now? (Yes)
- Ask for Clearing: I ask Archangel Michael to clear all energy associated with my ex-relationship in my Sacral Chakra. Clear and remove all forms of darkness, emotional, mental and at the cellular level. Thanks!
- Is the energy gone? (Yes)

So, ask until you feel you are ready and eventually you will learn to feel yourself when it lets go. Some sense when the energy is released, and others don't. It is perfectly possible to use a pendulum or just feel in case it is ready. It is important to know that dark energy is often connected to our fears, which means that the fears we have can be amplified when dealing with such energy. If you have a strong fear of working with spirituality, these feelings can be amplified by contact with dark energy. When we are completely free of that fear, the energy can no longer affect us in that area, because it no longer has any power over you.

In addition to what is mentioned above, you can also choose to have a daily routine where you cleanse, regardless of whether you feel any specific energy or not. Ask for help to clear all energy that is not yours and should not be there. When you ask guides for help, do so with empathy and trust that they will help you. It might sound like this:

"I ask Archangel Michael to clear all energy that is not mine and bring it back to its original source. Remove all lower energies until I am completely in my pure divine energy and power. I am in my light, I am free, I am divine."

Deeper Cleansing

If you have done what is stated in the previous part and still experience a lot of darkness, it may be that you have a lot of dark energy affecting you. Don't be afraid of it but know that this is only temporary and that you are always stronger than dark energies.

When we experience a large amount of darkness, so much so that we may be physically affected or feel stuck, we may need to dive a little deeper. We have seen patterns in ourselves and in clients that show we can experience a lot of darkness that originates in past lives. Many old souls have many tough lives behind them and if we carry with us a lot of trauma and deep-seated fears from previous lifetimes, we can be affected by a lot of darkness. It may sound very negative, but in the end, we only deal with things that we have been through, and we also create enormous power in ourselves through this work. By getting through this inner battle and getting to know all that we carry, we can help a great many people who come our way with similar difficulties.

To work with this, you can do the following:

- Find out where the energy comes from by asking questions.
- Am I affected by dark energy right now? (Yes)
- Where is this energy coming from, is it connected to someone I know? (No)
- Is it connected with the church or some ancient religion? (No)
- Is it connected to a past life? (Yes)
- Is it related to something traumatic that happened in that life? (Yes)
- Was I exposed to something? (Yes)
- Was it by a single person? (No)
- Was it some group or organization? (Yes)
- Was I in some sort of cult? (Yes)
- Was it a pure cult? (Yes)
- Was I exposed to violence in the sect? (Yes)
- Am I affected by the energy of the cult in this life? (Yes)
- Can I clear it? (Yes)
- Does this sit in any particular chakra? (Yes)
- Is it in the Root Chakra? (No)
- Third eye? (Yes)

Ask as many questions as you want, and you can use the pendulum or sense freely with intuition. Be aware of any feelings or fears that may come up as you work. When you do it this way, you access what is connected with the energy you feel. Then ask for help to release and clear the energy:

"I ask Archangel Michael, The Arcturians and my supreme guiding team of light to lift away fear, heaviness, pain, and darkness from past lives that affect me today. Help me heal cellular memories that no longer serve my highest good. I free myself completely from all forms of darkness that limit me. I choose myself and I choose the light!"

The more we go into our inner strength and security, the less we will be affected by external energies, in the same way that we are less affected by other people. When we feel good and have an inner calm, we handle people and events in the environment better and it is the same with energies from outside. YOU always have the power and the power in your life, no one else. The outside can only affect you if you allow it. So, work with self-love, inner security and pride - that's the best protection you can have.

Chapter 10

NEGATIVE ENERGY CORDS

In meeting people, energetic bonds or cords are created between us and those we spend time with. The more strong and intense feelings we have in contact with the other person, the stronger energetic bonds are often created. This means that when we have very positive, light, and loving feelings and thoughts about someone, a positive bond is created with the other person. When, on the other hand, we experience very strong negative emotions such as guilt, shame, anger or hatred, strong energy strings are created that have a very low frequency. Since we are basically social beings and always have more or less contact with other people, this means that we create such bonds all the time, often on an unconscious level. But since most conversations with other people are fairly neutral or relatively insensitive to us, these strings don't pose a problem. It is when we create deep emotional bonds or when we experience strong emotions connected with another person or place that heavier and more complex cords of energy are created.

We will look at an example of how negative energy cords can be created.

Maria is in a relationship with Jakob for 5 years. The relationship is quite stormy, and Jakob has problems with his alcohol addiction. He doesn't drink all the time but a lot on weekends and when he gets stressed or worried. Maria feels a lot of love and care for Jakob, and she does everything she can to help him. She is highly sensitive and senses and picks up on his bad mood a lot, which makes her despair.

She tries to get him to stop drinking, but every time she brings it up, Jakob feels questioned and gets very angry. This leads to Maria feeling strong guilt and she feels that she cannot do anything for him. This goes on for three years and the relationship ends when Maria decides to leave it. She still feels a lot of love for him, but as his drinking has escalated and he has started to withdraw, she feels that she cannot stay as it takes too much on her own well-being. The feelings Maria has after the breakup are failure, guilt, inner pain, sadness, and a feeling that she is not there for him anymore. How will he cope now? Time passes and Maria starts a new job and eventually meets a new guy. But even though she has in a way moved on, she thinks a lot about Jakob, how he is doing. She gets anxiety and sadness when she thinks about him and even though she tries to move on, it's like she keeps being drawn back to him and what they had, both mentally and emotionally. Since their relationship involved strong feelings, albeit both positive and negative, a lot of energetic cords were created between them. There are strong ties linked with guilt and failure. It is important that Maria becomes aware of these bonds and begins to dissolve them by clearing and by working with the emotions that come up.

Often, we have a lot of negative energy cords to people with whom we had a hard time or where the relationship has been unbalanced in some way. We can also have negative cords of energy in relation to our family members, because growing up it is common for us to experience both positive things and heavy things. To make it even more complex, we also pretty much always have past lives together with our family members and many of the partners we meet.

This means that we pick up old, ingrained patterns and behaviors when we meet these people in this life.

When we have sexual intercourse or intimacy with a person, we usually always create cords of energy with that person because we get close to them in different ways. Here it may be important to look at whether we had many partners or were with people we did not want to be with and clear away these energies. If you are in a relationship where you do not want closeness but still choose to have it, it can create strong negative bonds connected with the other person. If you have been beaten, abused or mistreated, either as a child or as an adult, there is a high probability that you may have created energy cords. In general, we can say that time matters - the longer we are in something dysfunctional, the deeper the bond is created and the harder it can be to get rid of it. But everything can be cleared away and let go of.

Why is it so important to clear negative Energy cords?
Negative energy cords usually have a very low frequency energy and when we have many such strings it will affect us negatively. It takes away our energy and we need all our energy to be able to create what we want and be in balance on all levels. Also, these low frequency emotions hold us back in various ways because we feel that we are not worthy of having a good time and so on.

If we look at the example of Mary; even though she partially moves on in life, she still experiences the feelings of guilt and failure. She will most likely carry those feelings and that energy into the next relationship if she doesn't deal with it. We often repeat the same pattern until we become aware of our inner self and heal, which is why Maria probably chooses to enter into an energetically similar relationship. Because she already carries these feelings of guilt and failure, she ends up in a new relationship where she gets the opportunity to deal with these feelings. For Maria, it is important that she works with her feelings of guilt and failure, for example through targeted healing and changes in external behavior. Our emotions are closely linked with our chakras. Guilt and failure have a strong connection with the Sacral Chakra and the Heart Chakra, our two relationship chakras. This means that it is valuable for Maria to work with these chakras.

Generally speaking, we can say that the stronger feelings we have towards something and the lower the frequency of these feelings, the stronger negative bonds are created. It doesn't matter if it's been 10 years since you had contact with an ex-partner or your mother, the energy bonds remain until you dissolve and release them.

Cutting negative Energy Cords

When we talk about cutting energy cords, it is always negative energy cords we want to cut and clear away. By negative we mean those with a low frequency that take energy, affect us negatively or hold us back in our development. Start by looking to see if there are any negative energy strands affecting you. Use your intuition or use a pendulum. Ask questions until you feel you have gotten what you want to know.

It could look like this:

- Are there any negative energy strands affecting or hindering me right now? (Yes)
- Is it connected with a person? (Yes)

- Were these cords created in this life? (Yes)
- Is that my mom? (Yes)
- Do they sit in any particular chakra? (Yes)
- Is it the Root Chakra? (No)
- The Heart Chakra? (Yes)
- Any more chakra? (No)
- Are they connected with any specific emotion? (Yes) Pay attention to what comes to you and trust it. Otherwise, ask further questions.
- Is it sadness? (No) Anger? (Yes)
- Can I clear them out? (Yes)
- Ask Archangel Michael (or your higher Guide Team) for help in clearing and cutting negative energy cords that exist between you and your mother, emotionally, mentally and on a cellular level.
- Ask for cleansing! Ask if that is enough for this time.

Sometimes it is enough to clear the energy immediately, but sometimes we may need to clear several times on different occasions. It is then often due to the fact that we have created very strong bonds for a long time or that we have strong feelings connected to the person that we have not really let go of (e.g. guilt, anger, sadness, etc.). Then we need to work with what is left. Mostly we feel pretty quickly if there is something there that we are not ready with. For example, if you get angry or a feeling of failure when you think about your ex-partner, then you can be pretty sure that it is precisely these feelings that are holding you back energetically. Think of it all as a process, the more you clear the more it will release. Be patient and be humble with yourself!

In addition to working with our chakras and clearing the energy, it is valuable to look at how we can change things in practical life. Create an awareness and understanding of your patterns and behaviors. Look at how you act in your closest relationships. Is there any area where there is a large imbalance? Do you feel small in relation to the other? Do you let yourself down? Do you feel guilt? By becoming aware of what is happening, you can also begin to change behavior and patterns that are actually not positive and that are limiting you. You may know by now that highly sensitive people and old souls very often diminish themselves and elevate those around them. If this applies to you, it's time to take back your power, step into your light, and take back power in your life.

To summarize:
- See if there are negative energy strands, either by asking or paying attention to feelings and thoughts connected with a particular person.
- Work with targeted healing and cleansing where you cut negative strings.
- Create an awareness of what your relationship patterns look like and try to change what does not give you energy and helps you develop.
- Remember that some energy bands can take a long time to clear, depending on how deep they are and how long they have been going on.

Chapter 11

SOUL CONTRACTS AND AGREEMENTS

What is a soul contract and how are these created? Soul contracts are energetic connections that have some similarities to negative energy cords. However, soul contracts are often a bit more extensive, and they can affect us a lot on different levels. A soul contract is an energetic contract that is created based on quite traumatic and difficult events in relation to other people. Of course, there is usually no physical contract, but it is pure energy.

Soul contracts are created based on the following circumstances:

- Through trauma in this or a previous life.
- Through strong emotional bonds with another person.
- Through strong patterns and through repetition over a long period of time.

Soul contracts are thus a kind of energetic binding, and they make us feel that we must act in a certain way or enter into certain roles/patterns. We can have a relationship with a person that we have had relationships within many past lives and that we meet again and again, not because we necessarily feel good about being with the person but because there are strong energy bonds and contracts involved. When we deal with and release these bonds, we free ourselves from the karma that exists, and we can then choose to continue being with each other or go our separate ways. It is common for old souls to be drawn into various forms of dysfunctional relationships and not infrequently it is because there are negative soul contracts we need to settle with.

Let's say you meet a man in this life to whom you feel a strong attraction. You meet and at first you feel that it works well, but soon notice that the man you live with treats you condescendingly. He has high standards of how you should be, and he makes you feel small. The longer time goes by, the worse things get between you. The man treats you downright badly and you become more and more afraid of him. He throws a tantrum and drinks, which makes it even worse. You don't feel safe with him, but still find it hard to break away. It's like something is holding you back, something is pulling you back to him even if you decide to leave. Finally, you manage to leave but after a lot of persuasion you go back to him again.

In a previous life, it turns out that you had a shorter relationship and that he exposed you to abuse. From that, a bond was created between you, a soul contract. This contract carries an energy of obedience and abatement. So, when you meet in the present life these feelings come up and you feel you have to do as he says. You feel that you don't have enough strength to get out of there, even though you know it's bad. To leave him in this life you need to see your own worth, stand up for yourself and start treating yourself with respect. By doing so, you will eventually put yourself and your health first and hopefully leave the man. But as long as we have these strong contracts, we can feel that we are stuck and that we are unable to get out of the situation. Since all this often happens unconsciously, it is valuable to look at what patterns emerge in our close relationships, especially if they are dysfunctional and make us feel bad.

The difference between soul contracts and negative energy strings is the intensity and that soul contracts are usually always caused by something traumatic. Negative energy strands can be created under slightly milder circumstances but still affect us greatly. We can have both soul contracts and negative energy strings with the same person. If you know that you are in a destructive or karmic relationship, there is a high probability that there may be both to work with.

A karmic relationship is a relationship where there is heavy karma between you and the other person. We distinguish between a relationship where there is karma and a purely karmic relationship. Many of the people we meet and form relationships with contain some karma from past lives. It is simply part of the journey we make as humans, to clear and release karmic patterns between us and other people. When it comes to a purely karmic relationship, there are often deep-seated problems and difficult karmic patterns between two people. These are people we have often met several times before and where the energy is very heavy, low-frequency and stagnant. Such a relationship causes us to hold ourselves back rather than lead us into development and joy.

Clearing Soul Contracts

We can clear soul contracts in a similar way as we work with negative energy cords. It is about creating an awareness and working with healing, cleansing and some change work. Feel in and ask if there is any contract affecting you right now, using your intuition directly or pendulum. There may be one, several or none that are current at the moment. If we don't get something now, we may meet one later, because we always get what we are ready for and need in the moment. Contracts can sit a little deeper than energy strings and often we need to go a little deeper, i.e. get clarity on what kind of contract it is. The reason for that is that contracts are often created based on rather difficult, traumatic and tough circumstances - which often last for a long time. Look at the questions below and use pure intuition or pendulum to answer.

Examples of how you can ask questions:
- Is there a contract right now that I should look at? (Yes)
- Was it created in this life? (No)
- Previous life? (Yes)
- Was I a woman in that life? (Yes)
- Was it someone I had a relationship with? (Yes)
- Have I met the person in this life? (No)
- Did we have a love affair? (Yes)
- Was it a happy relationship? (No)
- Was I afraid of him? (Yes)
- Did he subject me to any kind of violence? (Yes)
- Was a contract created out of this? (Yes)
- What is the contract about - that is, what feeling? Here you can feel in or use a pendulum. Is it anger? Fear? Feeling of not being listened to? Etc. Ask until you get a reasonably clear answer.
- Ask for help clearing and ending the contract. Here we usually use Archangel Michael and the Lords of Karma because they monitor and keep track of our karma and our past life experiences.

- Check so it's cleared by asking! If it can't be removed completely, clear some and come back again until you get it gone.

Remember that no question is wrong, just ask what you feel is relevant to you. After you work on the cleansing, trust that a process will start within you. The more you trust healing to happen, the more powerful it becomes. You may need to clear again for the same contract, as it is not always possible to remove everything at once. But every time you clear, more and more is released. Since every contract carries with it a certain energy, such as fear, uncertainty, guilt and so on, it is important to look at what patterns you have or have had with the person and change it. If you make yourself small with another person, practice taking up more space and standing up for yourself. The more you break free from the patterns that are negative, the more pure and balanced the energy between you becomes.

Agreements & Promises

While soul contracts are something that is created more unconsciously, agreements and various types of promises are somewhat more pronounced. It is something that we actually decide on or participate in under various circumstances.

Examples of agreements could be that we stated in a previous life that we should not devote ourselves to spirituality or that we should only follow the teachings of Christianity. In many past lives we have had fewer opportunities than today, and certain teachings and belief systems sit deep within us, perhaps because we have lived in them for a long time.

Examples of promises could be that in a previous life we were a monk or nun and thus made a promise to God. A promise not to engage in sexual acts, to live in chastity or celibacy. It may also be that we have been part of a sect or organization and made a promise to follow that type of faith. If we have been a monk in one life and vowed to live in celibacy, then in this life we may have a feeling that we are doing wrong when we are close to others intimately.

To clear & release Agreements

When we work with agreements and promises, our awareness is the most important thing. As soon as we become aware that we carry with us a promise from this or a previous life, it begins to dissolve. It may not release immediately but you are aware that it is there, giving you an opportunity to break these patterns, thoughts and feelings within yourself. It's easy to think that things that happened in past lives don't have much of an impact on our current lives, but the fact is, it's the opposite. Time is not linear as we perceive it here on earth, but everything happens parallel and circular. Events that happened in past lives affect us to the greatest extent here and now, especially if it involves strong beliefs or trauma. We have seen how a person who was a monk in a previous life had great fears about this in his current life. It is about fears connected with ethics and morality, not to do actions that go against God's will. In order to truly express our soul and to be able to work with our spiritual side in this life, we need to release and free ourselves from such forms of vows.

To clear and release promises/agreements, you can either feel free or ask questions with the pendulum:

- Do I have a promise that affects me right now? (Yes) Pay attention here to the first thoughts and feelings that come up in connection with this. Maybe there will be a certain feeling about something, an image or something that has limited you in this life.
- Does it come from my current life? (No)
- Previous life? (Yes)
- Does it have anything to do with authority? (Yes) Can apply to authorities, any organization or an individual.
- Does it have to do with any religion? (Yes) It's quite common for these types of promises to appear when we enter the spiritual path and especially if we are going to work on this.
- Is it connected with Christianity? (No)
- Any other religion? (Yes) You don't need to know exactly, it's enough to know roughly.
- Does it affect me most in any specific area? (Yes)
- The job? The family? Sexuality? Spirituality?
- Is it possible to clear this contract? (Yes)
- Ask your Higher Guide Team or Archangel Michael to clear this promise.
- You can say: "I ask my higher guiding team of light and Archangel Michael to clear this promise on all levels and existences. I completely free myself from this promise and go my own way in life."

Chapter 12

LOWER GUIDES

We have many helpers on the other side that we usually call our guide team. These can be guides that we lived with in previous lives or in other places in the Universe. Some guides have been with us since birth, while others come and go. As we enter more and more into our calling and as we make our inner journey, we tend to get more guides who back us up and support us. It seems quite natural that the more inner work we do and the more big events that happen in our life, the more assistance we need.

In addition to the guides who are with us in the form of deceased relatives or souls from our soul group, we can have a large number of angels, archangels and ascended masters that we receive help from and who help us in various areas. Some of these guides are with us without our knowledge and we can also choose to make contact ourselves and ask these high guides for help.

We usually only work with Archangels, Ascended Masters and Higher Light Guides in our work - because we feel it suits us best. Different guides can help in different ways and generally the guidance becomes somewhat more subjective the lower down in dimensions we go. This means that we may have deceased relatives on the other side who guide us and mean well, but because of their own fears and past life experiences, the guidance may be colored by their perspective. Archangels and ascended masters guide from a high and more objective level.

Sometimes we can have lower and more negative guides with us, and this often manifests itself through guidance and advice that is fear based, rather than light and love based. The highest purest guides will never tell you what is right, wrong, good or bad. They will also never accuse you or make you feel stupid or wrong. They always guide in a loving and Non-judgmental way. It's more like a whisper. "come this way" or "try this" or "take a step in that direction". So, if we receive guidance that tells us what we must do, what we must not do or that feels negative, then there are no positive guides helping us on our journey. For old souls, it is valuable to occasionally clear and upgrade their guides, this in order to have as clean and high guidance as possible. We can also have guides that we have "grown away from", that is, guides that have helped us a lot but that we no longer need because we have taken such big steps forward in our development.

To upgrade your Guide Team
Pay extra attention and see if there are lower guides around you if you notice that you are receiving guidance and direction that is fear based. If you receive guidance that is judgmental, that tells you that you are doing wrong, that you are not capable of what you are supposed to do and so on - then you are not being guided by higher beings of light. We can ask if we have any lower guides around us right now and if we do, ask for help in upgrading them to higher guidance. You can use pendulum if you are unsure about using your intuition completely freely.

Examples of how you can do:

- Be sure to clear the pendulum before asking, so that it is as clean as possible.

- Do I have any lower or negative guides affecting me right now? (Yes)

- How many is it? 1, 2, 3? Let's say you have two.

- Can I remove them and upgrade my guides? (Yes)

- "I am asking for help to upgrade my guide team to the highest good for me now. I only wish to have guides to help me move forward, closer to my soul and my life's mission!"

You can do this once a week or whenever you feel it is necessary. If you notice that your guiding feels weak, it is positive to do this.

Chapter 13

THE INNER CHILD AND YOUR CORE WOUNDS

When we move through our inner journey, one of the most important parts in our opinion is to work with the inner child, because this part of us affects our whole life and everything we do. It affects our view of ourselves, our major challenges and not least our relationship patterns. A damaged and unbalanced inner child can make our life a real roller coaster where we are constantly guided and act based on what happened in our upbringing, rather than based on where we are now. When it comes to strong soul relationships and Twin Flames, the most common reason for separation is precisely the inner child, that there are so many unhealed wounds within us that we cannot cope with being in the relationship. Either we cling to the other or we may find it hard to let go. By working with and healing the inner child, we open new doors and give ourselves an opportunity to be close to another person on a deep spiritual level.

But perhaps the most important thing of all is that we open the door to our heart and the relationship with ourselves. The relationship we have with ourselves is the one we navigate from during the course of life. If you have a deep and loving relationship with yourself, it will be reflected in all your relationships around you.

What is our Inner Child and how is it formed?

Our inner child is the part of us that is created and developed from the time in the mother's womb until adulthood. While growing up, we are incredibly dependent on the adults around us, and depending on what our growing up environment looks like, we will develop in a certain way. It cannot be emphasized enough how important this time is and the vast majority of people struggle with patterns, behaviors and emotions that originally come from their childhood. During the first years of life, a child is very open, receptive and sensitive to what is happening around him because it is during this period that the child begins to create his inner image of himself and other people. If this internal image is positive and balanced, the child will then very likely continue in this pattern and enter into balanced relationships as an adult. If the inner image says that other people are unreliable, that the world is dangerous or that you are not worthy of love, this will be reflected in relationships later on.

Young children cannot handle strong and overwhelming emotions on their own but need help from their parents in this. If the parents, in turn, carry a lot of fear and are emotionally unstable, they may not be able to face the child and help him deal with everything that is happening. This means that the child quickly learns to cope on his own and that there is no point in relying on other people. How should a parent who is afraid of his own feelings be able to meet the child's feelings? It will be an impossibility. If the child notices that the parent cannot meet his needs or feelings, he will probably perceive these as wrong and begin to shut down. Many empaths and highly sensitive begin at an early age to shut down their emotions in a way of survival as it becomes overwhelming to deal with everything that happens.

Many of us carry with us larger or smaller traumas from childhood that have become blockages in various ways. Maybe we were scolded without understanding why, maybe a parent disappeared without telling where they were going or maybe you had nightmares, but no parent listened or took you seriously. These may seem like small events, but to a young child they can be very frightening.

Of course, we can also carry with us major traumas such as sexual abuse, violence, abuse or a parent with mental illness. These things are often extremely frightening and traumatic for children. When a parent who is supposed to be the child's safe embrace becomes threatening, the child has nowhere else to turn but into himself.

Since growing up extends over a long period of time, we can have both isolated events that affected and still affect us today, but also ongoing events.

In psychology, it is usually said that our self is formed during growing up in interaction with the adults around us. Depending on how our parents treat us largely determines how we will treat ourselves. If you have a parent who constantly criticizes you or who thinks you take up too much space, as an adult you will generally be self-critical and find it difficult to take up space. If we grow up with a parent who has major emotional problems, we may learn to put our own needs aside for another person, because that's what we've done over and over again. In addition to our parents or those close to us, we are also influenced by others around us, such as friends and not to mention school time. School is a big part of our childhood and what happens there can leave a deep mark. If we feel left out or exposed to some kind of criticism every day at school, we as children pick up and integrate this as part of our inner being. How we handle what we have with us as children is closely related to how we are as people, our sensitivity and also our spiritual origin.

Who you are as an adult is a combination of everything you experienced in this and previous lives, both positive and negative.

What do we carry with us?

Our inner child is an energetic part within us, and everything remains there, both what is healed and what is unprocessed. All the events and feelings we experienced but which we could not handle or express are stored, as energy memories. Emotions are energy and when this energy is not allowed to move freely through the body but is blocked, blockages are created as previously mentioned. Much of what we carry from childhood lies on a deep unconscious level because it was a long time ago and because we may not remember it. Nevertheless, it goes on all the time within us and affects our life. When we experience something in the environment, we react with a feeling. If this feeling is very strong and we cannot deal with it, we have a defense mechanism, a part of our mind, that pushes the feeling down into the subconscious. This is a way for our body to protect us but because the feeling remains in the unconscious and vibrates at a low frequency (low emotions have a low frequency) we will attract people and situations based on this. We may attract a partner with the same problems we had during childhood. As we work to heal and release these blockages within us, we raise our energetic frequency. We will then attract new types of situations and people that match our new frequency.

Common problems that can come from childhood are:

- Sudden anger or rage
- Inner pain
- Fear of being rejected
- Fear of letting others in
- Severe anxiety/general anxiety
- Insecurity
- Guilt and shame
- Strong fears
- Feeling of not being sufficient as you are
- Major difficulties in relationships
- Big trust issues
- Physical problems
- Strong self-criticism
- Negative self-image
- Hard to like yourself
- Co-dependency
- Blocked heart
- Difficulty expressing emotions
- Excessively strong emotions
- Depression

To heal your Inner Child

Now we come to the part where we are to shower our inner child with love, attention and healing. All children need and long for unconditional love, to be seen and affirmed. We then look for the lack that is created in our upbringing throughout our lives - in close relationships, through work and through various external contexts. If we don't get love and security as children, a large part of our lives will be about just this. To heal our inner child, we need to give ourselves all that we lacked as children. Many times, we look for all that we lack outside of ourselves, but that is not where it is. External phenomena can give satisfaction in the moment but to truly create balance and inner harmony we need to create it within ourselves. The healing process with our inner child is not something we can skip, force or stress our way through. Think of it as a long and transformative journey, rather than something that can be solved at once. The more imbalances we brought with us from growing up, the more work we may have to do. Sometimes we have had a good and balanced upbringing but have experienced the occasional traumatic event. It can sometimes be easier to heal than when we lived under constant stress or trauma for many years. Security is precisely the basis for us to feel good, and if we have experienced a lot of stress while growing up, we may have to start there.

During our work with old souls, highly sensitive and starseeds, we have seen that many have difficulty seeing that they have actually been through trauma or carry heavy experiences with them. This is partly due to the fact that we often embellish events when we become adults or that we repress what we have been through. It could also be that you don't think you had it that hard, because you haven't been through anything that would outwardly be classified as trauma. But remember that trauma is always a subjective experience and something that is easy for others may be difficult for you. When we are highly sensitive, we are usually more affected by things in our environment and for a sensitive child, the fact that we don't feel seen for who we are, is a form of trauma in itself. Not infrequently we hear sentences like: "I had an alcoholic father, but it probably wasn't that bad" or "I had a pretty good upbringing, although I don't remember my parents having time for me or ever saying they loved me ". No parents are perfect and there are probably very few people who grew up with perfect balance. We are not here to judge our parents, but we need to see what happened through the eyes of the little child. As adults we may be able to understand why our parents acted the way they did, but as children we can't always. We are not supposed to go around being angry with our parents for the rest of our lives, for what happened back in the day (although that is also allowed). We need to deal with the feelings we carry, and we need to be able to express what has been suppressed and locked away.

Exercises to heal the Inner Child

The first step when it comes to any form of healing is to create an awareness of what you want to work with. In this case, it is valuable to create a greater awareness and understanding of how one's upbringing actually was. So, take some time and think about the following questions:

- Did I feel safe growing up?
- Was there stress or insecurity around me?
- How were my parents, physically & emotionally?
- Was there room for me to express what I wanted?
- Was there a lot of conflict?
- Did my parents (or other close adults) carry a lot of fear?
- Was there a traumatic event?
- Could I go to my parents if there was something?
- Did I feel a responsibility to either of my parents?
- How did my parents meet me emotionally?
- How was my schooling?

The following steps are about starting a dialogue with your inner child. By speaking to your inner child, you can see what it actually longs for and what it wants to express. You give the child the opportunity to be heard and come forward. If you find it difficult to do the exercise, take out a picture of yourself as a child. Have the picture in front of you and imagine that you, as an adult, are talking to the small child. Then start by feeling in and bringing up an event or a memory from childhood. It can also be a certain feeling. Don't be hard on yourself here but test yourself a little. It gets easier and easier the more you work with it. The aim is for you to bring out something from your childhood that affects you today and help deal with it. Such a dialogue with your inner child could look like this:

- I ask my guides to bring to me something about my inner child from childhood.
- I have a memory where my mother is very angry with me without knowing why. It makes me feel like a failure and I feel scared.
- I go into the feeling and ask my inner child what it wants to express and what it feels at that particular moment. I realize that I feel stupid and find it unpleasant with mother's anger.
- I ask my inner child if it wants to express something to mom and feel like I want to express the following: "I don't like it when you scold me, and I think it's unfair because I didn't do anything wrong!"
- Get into the feeling as much as you can in the meantime! If you can't feel anything, just trust that it will release anyway.
- When you feel that the little child has had the chance to express everything and when you feel that the emotions subside, you can think about what you, as an adult, want to say to the child.
- In this case, I choose to say and express out loud to my inner child: I understand that you are worried, but you can be completely calm. I am here for you, and you are absolutely amazing. I love you just the way you are, and you don't need to be afraid!
- In this exercise there is no right or wrong, but the important thing is that you start looking at what your inner child has

experienced, what it wants to say and start giving it exactly what it lacked.

- After you say what you want to say to the child - feel free to repeat loving things to yourself to reinforce this. Love has a high frequency and heals our inner wounds in a powerful way.

If you have difficulty finding or recalling a memory or a feeling, feel free to think about recurring patterns and negative emotions that exist in your life. It can be fear of being left, separation anxiety, fear of angry people, fear of letting someone in, a lot of anger towards others, a lot of criticism towards yourself or something else. Once you have found something that you want to work on, you can go in and have a dialogue with your inner child about that particular topic. Sometimes it may feel like you are making things up or fantasizing but let it be. Everything you do with this initiates healing within you, so dare to explore!

Additional exercise to heal your inner child:
- Sit or lie comfortably!
- Try to find a calm and let go of thoughts and feelings that come.
- Then ask Mary Magdalene and Archangel Raphael to provide healing for your inner child, where it is most needed right now.
- Just relax and pay attention to any feelings or energetic sensations in your body. Take deep breaths and trust that the healing will come in, exactly where it's supposed to.
- If you wish, you can express something like the following: "I am asking for the highest possible healing for my inner child. Help me access and heal old pain, grief or things that limit me.

If I carry inner resistance or protection, I ask for help to remove this, so that the healing happens more powerfully."

In addition to these exercises, it is incredibly positive if you notice situations where your inner child comes out. Look at what you have been through and think about what needs and behaviors it has created in you as an adult. If you notice that behaviors or patterns, come up in your relationships or in other contexts, work with healing, over and over until there is more balance. Remember that we may have to work with our inner wounds for many rounds before it eases and creates a more visible change in our life. Think about how you were as a child - what did you yearn for? Did you have dreams about something special? What did you like to do? Do things today that awaken the little child within you. See it as a tribute to yourself but also part of your healing and release. Everything you do where you get in touch with your playfulness, spontaneity and joy contributes to strong inner healing. Sometimes we see adults, even old people, who still have their childish minds. Many old souls take on so much responsibility early in life that it becomes a programming deep within us, a programming we have a hard time breaking out of, because it feels like we are doing something wrong.

Chapter 14

IMBALANCE OF THE
FEMININE AND MASCULINE

We all carry both feminine and masculine energy within us. These two energies are also around us in the Universe and existed even before we humans stepped down here on earth. The two opposite energies are also called Yin & Yang and we usually see them in a special symbol, a circle with black and white color where one part contains more of the black and the other half more of the white. Together they form unity and perfect balance.

Usually, men carry more of the masculine energy and women more of the feminine and this is what makes us perceive certain differences between men and women. These energetic differences and how we are shaped in the culture and society we live in create the gender roles we enter. It is nothing new that people on earth for a long time lived under patriarchy where the masculine energy dominated, and masculine characteristics were preferred over the feminine. Many of us today live more from our masculine energy because that's what we were taught to do, that's how we become successful and accepted. However, it is important to highlight that the masculine energy in its pure balanced form is neither dominant, oppressive nor superior. The masculinity mentioned above is an unbalanced form of the masculine created for the purpose of oppression and exercising power. In the same way that through millennia an unbalanced masculinity has been created, it has also happened to the feminine. The unbalanced feminine energy can manifest itself through martyrdom, conditioning, victimhood and excessive control. Neither the feminine nor the masculine energy is better or worse, they just are and when we have balance between them within us, we can function in harmony with ourselves and other people. We need to use both energies to achieve and live to our full potential.

What characterizes the Feminine and Masculine?

The feminine represents being, the intelligence of the heart, intuition, healing, our empathic ability, nurturing, vulnerability, unconditionality, motherhood and our emotions. It also stands for creation and dreaming, which means that everything within us is created first by the feminine. If we have an imbalance and deficit in our feminine energy or have difficulty releasing it, we can experience great difficulties in life. We may feel that we have difficulty creating something and that we are stuck. We find it difficult to feel our intuition and we may have too little contact with our feelings because we shut them down or do not access them. Maybe we find it difficult to be vulnerable and go into a lot of "I can handle everything myself". We can find it very difficult to calm down, to just be, to feel in and to be in quiet activities such as meditation.

If, on the other hand, we have an imbalance and excess of the feminine energy, we can instead experience that we are passive and that we have difficulty getting anything done at all. Maybe we get stuck in the dream stage all day without ever doing anything about it. We can also "drown" in our emotions and have difficulty handling all emotional impressions. We are only in the feeling without using common sense or our thoughts. We are constantly in our vulnerability and thus play a role of "victimhood".

The masculine represents thought, reason, intellect, action, to do, the brain, to realize and execute, fatherhood, to protect, organization and structure. It can be said that the masculine enacts and manifests what the feminine dreams of and creates within.

If there is an imbalance with a deficit in the masculine energy, we may find it difficult to get things done and our thoughts may run sluggishly. We may have a hard time organizing things and we don't really get things done. We start projects but are unable to follow through and complete. We can also let others treat us badly because we don't use our fatherly energy to actually protect ourselves.

An excess of masculine energy manifests itself in the fact that we constantly perform, are active, find it difficult to be still and we are constantly in the brain. We think and analyze rather than using our feelings and our intuition. We organize things around us and have great demands on us to manage as many activities and things as possible in the shortest possible time. We streamline things and rarely stop to feel how something feels. Maybe we're not even in touch with our emotions anymore because we're so used to being up in our heads through our thought processes.

The last example of masculine excess shows how we humans live in large parts of the world, perhaps even more so in the Western world. That's because it's still the dominant norm. The vast majority today, BOTH men and women, live predominantly in their masculine energy. They do, perform, act, think and organize their entire existence, not least in workplaces where this is seen as a matter of course. But our body is not created to only be in the masculine energy, which means that it will eventually collapse - what we call burnout today. The reason more women burn out may be because women are not created to live in masculine energy in the same way as men, which means their bodies collapse and take even more of a beating from today's social structure. Women (and men) are created to live in balance between these two energies and when there is instead a large imbalance it affects the individual but also the whole society. A social apparatus is created that is made for men and the softer and feminine qualities are seen as a weakness or something wrong. Women thus do everything they can to try to cope with doing "right" and living according to the masculine structure. However, we want to emphasize that this is very general and that some men have more dominant feminine energy and vice versa.

A balanced dance between the feminine and masculine means:
- Balance between thought and feeling
- Balance between brain and heart
- We dream and we execute
- We create and we manifest
- We are and we do
- We protect and we care
- We are vulnerable and we are powerful
- We organize and we fantasize

To have a little imbalance during certain periods of life is completely in order and normal. Sometimes we may need a little more of our masculine energy, for example when we need to act quickly and be powerful. Sometimes we need more of our feminine energy, for example when we have a great need for rest and calm. It is when the imbalances become long-term patterns and when we live based on the imbalanced every day, that it can have negative consequences. In Twin Flame relationships or other strong soul relationships, we usually need to work a lot on balancing our feminine and masculine in order to be in balance with each other. It is part of the journey you make together and if there are major imbalances here, it will quickly show between you and your partner. Your partner will reflect exactly what you need to work on within yourself. For example, if you find it difficult to meet your feminine energy and your inner vulnerability, your partner may go into his vulnerability a lot. This can then arouse irritation or fear within you because the vulnerable is something you do not want to see/experience in yourself and therefore not in the other person either. Another example is if you were not listened to as a child. Your Twin Flame or partner will then most likely exhibit behavior patterns of not listening, which will drive you crazy. We need to examine these aspects within ourselves and gain more balance where there is trauma or old wounds.

In Twin Flame relationships or strong soul connections, it is common for one partner to carry more feminine energy and the other more masculine energy. It is something that is predetermined and by triggering old blockages and imbalances in each other you help each other heal on a deep and spiritual level. Most of the time, it is the man who carries more of the masculine energy, but not always. The partner with more masculine energy often has strong inner protection, blockages connected with the heart, more difficulty being in touch with their heart and emotions and a tendency to escape. These aspects are closely related to the inner wounds created in the masculine both in individuals but also over millennia in society.

177

The person with more feminine energy often exhibits an imbalance in the form of "needing" the other, holding on and trying to control the other person or relationship. Generally, the person with more masculine energy needs to surrender, open up his heart and his vulnerability and dare to face himself and thus the other. The person with more feminine energy needs to create stability within oneself, let go of control and build up inner security and trust. A nice parable about the feminine and the masculine is the story of Jesus and Mary Magdalene. We do not look at Jesus from a religious perspective, but rather we see him as a divine figure and a great Healer. Based on what we have been told about Jesus and Mary Magdalene, they were Twin Flames, which means that they had a strong spiritual relationship. Together they form a perfect balance for the feminine and masculine within us. Mary Magdalene was the one with the most feminine energy and helped and supported Jesus, while he was the one who accomplished much in the exterior.

As I said, we all have both a feminine and a masculine energy within us and the further we get on our spiritual journey, it is important to become aware of and strive for balance within these two energy aspects. Think of it as you have an inner man and an inner woman within you and these two need to come more and more into balance, both within themselves and with each other. A good way to work with this is to investigate if there is a large imbalance within any of the energies and try to create more balance where needed.

Imbalance in the masculine

As previously mentioned, our masculine energy stands for practical action, thought, logic, thoughts, common sense and protection. So, have a look at if you struggle with the following:

- Stress and a lot of activity.
- You are very much in your thoughts and analyze everything.
- Difficulty perceiving or accessing your feelings.
- You feel closed off or have difficulty getting in touch with your inner self and your intuition.
- You have a lot of "performance thinking" in your everyday life.
- You have a hard time being still.
- You easily get a bad conscience if you do nothing.
- You have a hard time entering into your vulnerability.
- You have a strong resistance to facing your inner self.
- You go into defense a lot, that is, defend yourself against others and the outside world.

If you have one or more of the above points, it may mean that you have an imbalance in your masculine energy, which means that there may be a deficit or excess in the energy. Feel free to look at how you can create balance in these areas. Examples of what you can do is to go more into your feelings, go into stillness and being, slow down, feel and experience your feelings. You can also work on getting in touch with your intuition, dare to be vulnerable and find a way to calm your thoughts in everyday life. All of these are different ways you can work to create more balance.

It is valuable to strive for balance between different parts of life such as:

- To give and take
- The inner and outer
- To do and to be
- To think and to feel
- Using intellect and heart
- To create and manifest

As previously mentioned, our feminine energy stands more for our softer qualities such as care, love, vulnerability, creation, the heart, emotions, being, stillness and intuition. So please take a look if you struggle with one or more of the following points:

- Passivity and difficulty getting started.
- Shut down creativity.
- Feeling that you are "drowning" in your emotions.
- Feeling of victimhood and a lot of exposure.
- Difficult to stand up for yourself in, for example, relationships.
- Codependent problem.
- Very emotional.
- Caught up in dreams and longing without moving forward.
- Creates a lot within you but doesn't get it out in daily life.

Here you can work with, for example, converting creation into physical manifestation, moving physically, getting things started on a practical level and learning to manage your emotions in a constructive way. It is also valuable for you to set clear boundaries and stand up for yourself, moving from feeling to action and turning your vulnerability into strength within you.

A simple exercise to balance your energies
Feel free to ask your guides or your higher self to upgrade, balance and heal your inner feminine and masculine energy – your inner man and woman. When we addressed the inner child in previous chapters, we described how the inner child is an energetic part or sub-personality that exists within us and that affects how we act and behave. See your inner man and woman in the same way, as two parts within you that may have experienced injury, stress or trauma. While our inner child is influenced by our upbringing, our inner man and woman are greatly influenced by our past lives and also the collective one. If you have had several lives as a woman where you have been subjected to abuse or experienced trauma due to being a woman, these may sit as energetic memories within you. Maybe you were a man in a previous life and were forced into war, even though you didn't want to. In the war you died and lost your pride as well as your whole family. This can damage our masculine part within us, and we can experience remnants of that energy here and now.

To balance and heal your feminine & masculine energy, you can take help from your higher guide team. We give examples here of which guides you can use, but of course you can take help from those you want. We have chosen Archangel Michael and Mary Magdalene, because they are two powerful symbols of the feminine and the masculine. Maria Magdalena has a wonderful feminine and caring energy, and her healing goes straight to where it is needed when you ask for it. Archangel Michael carries a strong and protective masculine energy, which makes it positive to use in this inner work. Trust that you get the help you need and that the healing is directed to where you need it most to take the next step forward. Your right part of the body represents your masculine energy and the left part your feminine energy.

Do the following to work with healing:

- Sit or lie down comfortably and take a few deep breaths. Ask Archangel Michael and Mary Magdalene to come to you and to be with you in your healing work.
- Set a clear intention for what you want to do, for example to balance and heal your inner feminine and masculine energy. If you have a specific area, please express here what you would like help with. Remember, there can never be too much. They help you as much as you want and ask for, always.
- Then express: "*I now ask Archangel Michael to balance and heal my masculine energy, my inner man. Help me release and heal cellular memories from past lives and events in this life that affect me or hold me back.*"
- Feel free to sit for a while and feel if you experience anything. If not, just focus on your breathing.
- Then you move on to your feminine part. "*I now ask Mary Magdalene for the greatest possible help to balance and heal my inner feminine energy. Help me release and heal cellular memories and current life events that affect me or hold me back.*"
- Now ask for help to integrate your feminine and masculine energy within you so that they create a balanced unity. You can

also ask for help to upgrade your inner man and woman. It may sound like this: *"Now help me to integrate and balance these two energies with each other so that they create balance within me. Upgrade my inner man and woman to the highest possible level."*

- Feel free to imagine energy flowing down through your body and trust that the healing is happening.
- If you want, thank for the healing when it's done!

Chapter 15

An imprint is a created truth, i.e. an idea about something we have created through various events and experiences. As children, we are very open and when we are very young, we do not know what is right and wrong. It is something we learn through the interaction and interaction with our surroundings. We build up patterns, ideas and imprints based on what we are involved in. We can have individual events that create imprints, but it can also be related to a longer course of events. We will now cover some different types of conditioning, so that you get an idea of how they can look and shape us.

Conditioned allergy

Conditioned allergy means that we develop an allergy, or a phobia based on a certain event. Let's say you're being mistreated during breaks at school, maybe even bullied by other students. After the break, you go into the cantina and drink a glass of milk. Because at that very moment, when you drink the milk, you may have these feelings of discomfort in your body, you make an unconscious connection between what happened and the milk. All of a sudden, you can't drink milk anymore, but every time you want to drink, you get a strong discomfort or fear. Your body associates' milk with danger and this then becomes a created truth that we continue to live by unless we become aware of what caused it all and heal it within ourselves.

Progressed Conditioning

A progressed conditioning can be created when we repeatedly experience negative or unpleasant consequences, based on something that happens. Imagine that you grow up in a family where it is considered wrong to be sad. Quite a few people can probably recognize this more or less. Every time you get sad or cry, it has negative consequences for you. Your father gets angry and calls you oversensitive. He thinks you should know better than to behave that way. This creates an inner truth, or an imprint. It is wrong to be sad and you try to avoid it at all costs in life. It can make you feel uncomfortable every time you feel sad or even if someone else around you shows feelings of sadness.

Generational conditioning

These are imprints that we get with us from a parent who in turn got it from their parent and so on. It can be deep-rooted truths and beliefs about how things should be and how we should live to get love or to simply survive. An example of that is a notion that it is negative to have a lot of money. Because you have this built-in truth within you, it becomes difficult for you to make much money. Maybe you earn a certain amount but notice that it reverses every time you start pulling in more money. There is a glass ceiling that prevents you from reaching the stars. This means you need to free yourself from this imprinting and remove the glass ceiling so you can create and manifest your own way in life. Imprints like this often sit unconsciously within us.

Conditioning from past lives

We can also carry with us imprints and patterns from past lives, which we carry with us energetically in our cells and chakras. These imprints mean that we are sometimes drawn back into the same situations, events and relationships because it feels familiar and familiar to us. We can also think things are wrong without understanding why. Maybe you have had a life connected with a certain religion and in this life, you have a hard time with that religion. Just hearing about it you feel strong resistance, without having any experience of it in the present life.

As you can see, there are quite a few different types of conditioning, and a lot goes into each other in different ways. The important thing is to start accessing and seeing what you carry so you can start reprogramming and upgrading yourself and parts of your life. Don't get stuck in which imprint it is but choose what feels right or what you think matches yours.

Release Imprints

Imprints are inner truths, programming or beliefs that affect us daily, often without us even being aware of them. In order to live more and more in accordance with our divinity and our soul, we need to review and clear away what actually limits us in the form of created perceptions. When we reach the age of 20, we are often so shaped by parents and surroundings that we do not know who we are behind all this. We have taken on a variety of psychological and social codes with which we identify.

For example, it could be things like:

- I am an insecure and shy person
- I cannot eat certain types of food
- I have a hard time with social life
- I'm weird
- I can't handle things
- I have to be nice to be liked
- I'm not creative
- I have no direct talents
- I don't have what it takes to succeed
- I don't fit in the world
- I'll never get on
- I am stuck
- I can't make money
- I cannot create success
- I have bad health
- I am a bad person
- I should handle things better
- It's wrong to be sensitive

There are any number of things to highlight here and as long as we have such imprints within us, THEY are the ones who control us, not our divinity and inner power. The truth is that you are a powerful, eternal, loving and creative soul - no matter what you've been through or what you feel. No one can take that away from you. The important thing here is to become aware, to really look at how you live and how you view yourself, life and the environment.

Analyze it and see if you are living the way you long to live. Ask yourself the following questions:

- Am I living my highest best life right now?
- Am I who I want to be now?
- Am I doing what I long for and that awakens my passion?
- If not - what do I need to do to get there?
- Which of my beliefs stop me in this?

For example, if you have a notion that says you can never earn money, because you were born into a family with poor finances - then that is exactly what you will create. What you think and feel daily creates your reality. As long as you are convinced that you cannot make money, you CANNOT make money. It goes against our universal laws. You need to shift your inner belief, your energy, your thoughts and feelings until you KNOW you can make money.

If you have a medical condition, an allergy or something else you struggle with, look at what's behind it. Our allergies are created many times by events where we experience fear, fear that we do not have the ability to process in a positive way. This energy and fear set in as an allergy and when you access the event itself and the emotions connected to the event you can get rid of the allergy altogether. So, if you have a strong fear or phobia about something, try to get to what's behind it. Use the pendulum or feel in with intuition:

- Let's say you have a milk allergy.
- Was the allergy created in this life? (Yes)
- Which age? 1? 2? 3? 4? Etc.
- Did something special happen then? (Yes)

- Here you can see if any memory, feeling shows up or you can ask more questions. We continue to use the same example as before. Say that you recall a memory where you were exposed to something difficult at school. You were teased in the schoolyard in front of other children. Afterwards you went in to eat and you were under a lot of stress. You ate food and drank milk. The combination of milk, inner turmoil and stress created a sensitivity or reluctance for the body to drink milk.

- Go into and experience any feelings and thoughts that come up. Allow anything or nothing to come. Everything is okay.

- When you have found the cause and gone into the feeling as much as possible, ask for help to heal and heal feelings connected to this. You can ask your higher self, guides, or the angels for help. Trust that you will get the help you need.

- If you want, you can also see yourself in the situation where the event took place and imagine how you handle the situation in a new way - you recreate the energy and the course of events. See how after the incident you go inside and find peace within yourself, feeling safe and loved.

You can also look at what thoughts you have about finances, self-worth, your personality, job and relationships. Every truth that you create within becomes your truth on the outside. Everything you see around you is a reflection of what you carry inside.

If we take finance as an example. Ask yourself what you think and think about this? Is there any limitation? If there is something there that you find, you can for example look at the following:

- Let's say you feel it's hard to get enough money together
- Did this imprinting occur in this life? (Yes)
- Does it come from one of my parents? (Yes)
- Dad? (No)
- Mother? (Yes)
- How many generations ago was it created? (3)
- How does the conditioning affect me? Does it affect me in any particular chakra? Mentally? Emotionally? (Mentally and emotionally)
- Ask for help to clear and remove this conditioning! You can suggest the help of Archangel Michael.
- Then go in and transform the energy here by building new beliefs within you. You can imagine yourself with a lot of money while entering a positive and empowering energy. Think thoughts like you create everything you want, that you have plenty of money, that you live in abundance, that you are powerful and that you are WORTHY of having a good economy.
- So, see yourself where you want to be and the more you can see, feel and experience as if you are already there the more powerful it will be. Here you transform the energy into the energy you want to be in.

Chapter 16

FEELINGS, THOUGHTS AND BEHAVIOR

We all have complex parts and patterns within us that together build our thoughts, feelings and behaviors in everyday life. These building blocks are part of being human here on earth. We can't opt them out, but we can change them. We can become aware and transform these aspects so that they more closely match our higher energy, our heart and who we want to be.

Our Feelings

Emotions are a part of life and although many find it challenging to manage this particular area, life without emotions would be flat and boring. It is through our emotions that we experience the world around us, both all the fantastic and more burdensome things. We are not our feelings, but our feelings are something we have brought with us in our physical existence. See it as a kind of tool to be able to navigate through life.

Emotions are pure energy and what we experience when the energy passes through our body is precisely what we call emotions. What determines whether the feeling is pleasant or unpleasant is the frequency at which the feeling vibrates. The lower the frequency of a feeling, the more heavy and challenging it can be experienced in our body. The higher the frequency a feeling vibrates at, the more lovely and easy it will feel. Examples of emotions that have a low frequency are shame, guilt and anger. There is probably no person who wants to feel those feelings precisely because they are experienced as troublesome and heavy for us. When we have a lot of locked heavy emotions in our body, they create heaviness, fatigue and a sluggishness for us. We lose our energy, and we constantly feel tired and stiff in the body. Locked emotions keep the low energy inside us, constantly vibrating and in external situations this feeling is triggered - not to hurt us but to show us that it is something we need to look at. When we look at, meet and heal the feeling, that energy is released from our energy system, and we rise in frequency. This means that the more emotions we process and release, the more we can rise in frequency and move towards higher dimensions. This is exactly what happens in our ascension process - we are forced to face a lot of darkness to make our way towards the light.

Examples of Emotional Blockages

Imagine that as a child you are craving sweets and decide to try to take some sweets that you know are hidden in the pantry at home. Just as you take the candy off, your dad appears behind you and starts yelling at you. You get really scared and startle. He scolds you and says you should be ashamed. A strong sense of shame is awakened within you that you find difficult to deal with, which makes you try to do everything you can to get rid of it. The feeling is pushed down into the unconscious and you immediately find that it feels a little easier. The problem now is that this feeling of shame has become locked up in your emotional body. It now lies there and vibrates all the time on an unconscious level. As our body and soul are constantly striving for balance and towards inner healing, you will have the opportunity to release this feeling. How? Well, because something triggers the feeling at a later time. 3 years later, you might find yourself in a situation where someone behaves in a similar way, which awakens this feeling of shame within you. You can then either choose to run away and thus push down even more shame or you can choose to face it and experience it until it releases and leaves your system.

The example of the candy may seem like a simple event, but it is often these types of energy and emotional blocks that we have. Imagine then how much we are affected by major and traumatic events such as abuse, violence or mental imbalance in our parents. The more strong emotions we push down, the harder it can be to bring them up and face them, precisely because they have been intensified for a long time. But no emotion is dangerous, but what prevents us from facing emotions is often our own fear of the emotion in the belief that it will hurt us. We can create a huge resistance to facing emotions and sometimes we dissociate ourselves from them completely, meaning we don't even know we have them. We may find it difficult to access them because we have completely disconnected ourselves from them. Many highly sensitive people have a tendency to avoid emotions from an early age because they feel so much and strongly that it simply becomes overwhelming.

Another example of emotional blocks are those that are created for a long time because we deny or do not have the opportunity to feel a certain emotion. If we learn growing up that it is bad and wrong to be angry, we may start to avoid anger, especially if it previously led to negative consequences for us. It gradually leads to us accumulating a lot of anger inside us that we have not been able to express and feel. Some we meet say that they never get angry or can feel anger, but according to us, anger is one of the emotions that are part of being human in a physical body. Everyone gets angry at some point in the same way that everyone gets sad or happy at times. If we don't have access to anger at all, it may be because we have hidden the feeling away so much that we don't actually think it exists. If we do not get an outlet for our anger when we are children, especially if we are exposed to some kind of trauma or similar, our repressed anger can turn into rage. Rage is anger that has somehow become distorted and amplified precisely because of our unbalanced approach to it. Many people are ashamed of anger and believe that anger in particular is something wrong because they have been taught that at home and in society. It is many times easier to be sad and being sad can be more accepted by others than being angry. All emotions are healthy in their pure form and since emotions are just energy, they cannot be right or wrong - they just are.

Mental Blockages

Our thoughts, in the same way as our feelings, are a tool we have as humans here on earth. When we learn to understand and master our thoughts, they can be a great gift and asset to us. Through our thoughts, we can plan, structure and move forward in life in a purposeful and powerful way.

When we work with our inner self, we usually need to examine both feelings, thoughts and behaviors because these three parts are connected. We experience a feeling and think something and then act in a certain way.

Blockages in our thoughts can express themselves in many different ways. When we have repeated thought patterns and when we find it difficult to break certain thoughts, we may have some type of blockage, that is, the energy has stagnated or become blocked precisely in the subject in question.

We can also experience thought blocks that manifest in fear of our thoughts. Maybe then we are afraid to think about certain subjects. This in turn can cause us to avoid thoughts, which makes us limited in life.

Mental blocks can cause us to stay in old patterns due to fear and we can have thoughts that hold us back on different levels. Imagine that you decide to start working in the spiritual field, but every time you approach your start-up, the same thought comes: "I will never be able to do this" or "I am not spiritual enough". We need to work on healing feelings within us but also on breaking and replacing negative thought patterns. We often think the same thoughts many times a day completely unconsciously, things that we have learned about ourselves and others. There are researchers who believe that we don't really think for ourselves at all, but that 90% of our thoughts are pre-programmed and rehearsed. We think the same thing as we thought yesterday and the day before and so we continue in this way until we become aware and choose to think anew. We cannot create new and expand by thinking in an old way that did not work for us.

As long as we believe and think that we can't do something, we can't. Our body listens to our thoughts and eventually what you think becomes a programmed truth for you.

Thoughts, like feelings, are pure energy, and by thinking positively and empoweringly about yourself, this positive energy is directed towards you and what you create - you move forward. Breaking old thought patterns is often challenging and it requires courage and determination, as with everything else on our inner spiritual journey.

The more you work on thinking lovingly about yourself, the easier and faster you move forward on your journey. Low thoughts about yourself hold you back and drag you down in frequency.

We often come into contact with people in our work where challenges with thoughts occupy a large part of their everyday life. It can be limiting thoughts, doubts, fears and thoughts that prevent them from moving forward. Our experience is that mental blocks can sometimes be even tougher to work with than emotions. It depends on several factors. As highly sensitive, you are extremely sensitive to what goes on around you growing up. If it becomes too overwhelming emotionally, there is a risk that you "shut down" your emotional body and live in your head instead. You live through your thoughts and if there are strong fears there your life becomes limited and square. It also creates an overactivity in the Crown Chakra where you experience confusion or disconnection from your emotions and your intuition.

Behind blockages in our thoughts are often strong emotional blockages. When we dare to go beyond our thoughts, we find the root cause, what makes us feel blocked in thought.

Behavioral Blockages

Sometimes we get stuck in behaviors that are not good for us and it can be well worth examining these. Most of our actions are guided by our feelings - we either want to achieve a feeling or avoid a feeling. We want to feel love or avoid being hurt. We learn during our first years of life how to behave in order to be loved and seen. Based on that, we act and make our way through life's challenges.

Here, it can be important to look at how you behave and act to gain more clarity on what is going on. Do you have a behavior where you often run away from your inner self or from conflicts? Are you acting out of fear of abandonment? Our behaviors say a lot about what we carry and where our deepest inner wounds are.

Stop and observe how you act towards your partner, a parent, and so on. By breaking dysfunctional behaviors, you can access what is behind such a troublesome feeling. Maybe there is sadness, pain or anger behind the action you take. We may stay in relationships even though we know we should leave them. This is something we have done for as long as we can remember, and it doesn't matter that we know it intellectually. The reason we choose to stay is because we don't dare to face the pain and feeling of abandonment that lies behind it. So, we stay there even though we feel worse and worse. Perhaps this fear comes from childhood where we were often abandoned by our parents, which brought a feeling of abandonment.

Heal the Triangle of Feelings, Thoughts & Behavior

When we look at how we handle situations in life, we can often see a pattern of our feelings, thoughts and behavior. We experience an external event that evokes a feeling that creates certain thoughts and which in turn causes us to act in a certain way. Here it can be important to work with all three parts.

Imagine you are conversing with a family member, in this case your mother. She mentions that you've been single for way too long, which makes you angry. You experience anger and you feel questioned. Actually, your mom means well but the way she says it makes your whole body react and go into defense. You feel angry and think that your mother is so critical of you, so you leave and slam the door. This can also be explained in terms of a trigger, that you are triggered by something. The term Trigger can sometimes be overused and thrown around almost as a swear word. But it is important to know that behind a trigger is often a trauma or unprocessed inner wound. People and situations that make us react strongly awaken something within us. Here, our inner child or events that we carry and that we still haven't dealt with are activated.

So, what can you do?
In the same way that you work with your chakras and the inner child, you can become aware, stop and look at what is happening within you. By taking responsibility for what is happening inside you, you can also heal it. As long as it is on the outside, it is beyond your control, but as soon as you see what is happening inside you, you have the opportunity to really let it go. Of course, there can be things on the outside that are wrong in various ways and sometimes people do things that are anything but loving. But the only thing you can take responsibility for and do something about is yourself. When you change something within yourself, you soon notice that others begin to behave differently towards you. When you change the energy within you, others must respond to you in a different way, this according to the law of attraction.

Choose a situation & look at the following:
- What is happening in the situation?
- What feelings does it evoke in you?

- Do you recognize these feelings? Have you known them before and when?
- When did these feelings arise? Feel in or use a pendulum!
- Feel the emotions as they come as much as possible.
- Feel free to find where in the body they sit - are they in the stomach? The legs? The head? The back?
- When the feeling subsides, ask for help to release the feeling. Feel free to ask your higher self, a guide or an angel for help in the process. Have confidence!
- Also feel free to look at your thoughts - what kind of thoughts are coming? Can you change your thoughts and think something empowering and healing? Important to break certain thoughts that recur and are not helpful to us. Keep in mind that all patterns we break can take some time, as can habits and behaviors. Have patience!
- In terms of behavior or action – can you do any other way? Can you practice staying in the situation a bit? Not to leave immediately, but to stay and see what happens.

This work requires awareness and that you are truly willing to work with and examine what is going on within you. But you are ready for this! Dare to challenge yourself and go behind the exterior.

Take a piece at a time
If you feel that it is getting confusing or if you have difficulty knowing where to start, practice on one thing at a time. Start by observing your emotions in different contexts. As long as we have a lot of unprocessed emotions within us, we are usually emotionally

controlled - that is, we react a lot to things on the outside. Or it is the other way around, that we feel disconnected and numb. Both conditions are signs that we have much unprocessed within us. The more we heal within, the more we can relate in a calm and harmonious way to the outside, because we know that the only thing, we can really do something about is our inside. You can start with a single emotion in your life if you want. Find a feeling that you yourself experience hinders you or affects you negatively. Then be aware of when this feeling appears in different contexts. It may be that you experience sadness when watching television or when meeting other people. What does this sadness stand for? What does it come from?

Use pendulum or feel in:

- When did I start feeling this feeling?
- Is it connected with a certain event?
- Where in the body is it located? (for example, the Heart Chakra)
- It may be that the feeling of sadness comes up (it doesn't have to).
- If you feel the sadness, allow it to come and feel it until it starts to subside. Maybe other feelings come up, let them come up and work with them.
- Focus on the heart and ask your higher self and higher guides for help to heal and release this feeling.
- For example, you can say: *"I am now asking my highest guidance team for help to heal this feeling at the cellular level. I allow myself to experience the sadness and then let it go"*.

Chapter 17

PAST LIVES AND CELL MEMORIES

In this part of the book, we will delve into Past Lives. We can also refer to our past lives as parallel lives, because linear time does not exist as we see it here on Earth. Some carry with them memories or glimpses of past lives. We can get information about past lives through our dreams, through specific events and places we are drawn to or vice versa, things we feel strong resistance to without knowing why. If you have a strong attraction to Ireland without knowing why, you have most likely lived a life there, a relatively good life. If, on the other hand, you feel a strong resistance to the place without having been there, it may be that you lived a tough life there in another incarnation.

We can also feel drawn to certain eras that run through history, for example we are extremely interested in the French Revolution. Then it could be a clue that you lived during that time. The energy we carry within us is passed on via our soul and via our etheric body and as soon as you are in a new body, you carry this energy with you in your cell memories. When you are ready, external events in this life will trigger exactly what you need to be whole and heal on all levels.

When we go from life to life, we take with us everything energetically, everything we have experienced and everything we have left to process. This means that unresolved events from the past can come up as a current theme in this life. Let's say that in your past life you lost your child in a terrible accident. Because you lived in a chaotic and stressful environment, you were not given the opportunity to process the trauma of your lost daughter. You shut down your sadness and a deep blockage is created in your heart. In your current life, you have a strong anxiety that something terrible will happen and you have a closed heart. You don't open it up to anyone and just the thought of having a baby makes you panic. This comes up in this life to give you another chance to process the trauma you previously experienced.

Another example is that you were sexually abused by your husband in a previous life. The abuse went on for a long time and caused a deep trauma within you. The energy settled as blockages in your Sacral Chakra (chakra for our sexuality) and in the Heart Chakra (trust in other people). In the current life, you have difficulty trusting men and you feel closed off when it comes to sexuality. Since the problem arose in previous lives, it is not possible to work with events only from this life. It is important that we look at the present but that we have an openness to the fact that a certain problem can extend far back.

If you have major and recurring problems and challenges in this life without being able to trace them to your upbringing or any specific event, the probability is high that this was with you even before birth. The very biggest challenges we have in this life are almost always a continuation and a consequence of something we started in previous lives. Our core problems, or Core issues, we have worked with for several lives. Therefore, we need to be humble towards ourselves and towards other people and know that everyone is doing the best they can based on where they are right now. Time doesn't really exist, at least not in the way we think here. On earth, we are very dependent on counting everything in time and space, but from a spiritual perspective, there is really only the present. This means that our so-called past lives are energetically just as present and affect to the same degree as what happens in this life. Your body cannot distinguish between time, but it feels the vibration of what is going on and strives for healing.

7 common Events that affect us from Past Lives
In our work, we have seen 7 common past life events that affect many old souls. These are events that created trauma and that create limitations in various areas today. We highlight them for you to look at if there is something you recognize in your life.

1. We have been killed because of our spirituality or our beliefs, which makes us feel resistance or fear to work with spirituality in our current life.
2. We have had a lot of power and abused it, making us afraid of our power in our current life.
3. We have been tortured or exposed to a violent death, for example through war, which makes us afraid to face both internal and physical pain.
4. We have been silenced and diminished by authorities, causing us to follow orders and find it difficult to go our own way in this life.
5. We have had lives like slaves or serfs, where we were forced to work hard for little or no money. This means that we live in scarcity and find it difficult to create money and abundance.
6. We have been exposed to sexual abuse, which affects our sexuality in our current life.

7. We have been extremely poor and, in some cases, died from material lack, which creates a feeling that we must hold tight to material things and sometimes even food.

Healing Energy from Past Lives

Healing blockages from past lives is not really that different from healing things that happened in our childhood because everything we experienced is stored energetically within us. This means that it is equally important to work with all the parts. Our soul remembers everything we've been through, all the incarnations we've ever had. Here you can work in a similar way as we covered in the previous chapter. You can use your pure intuition, use a pendulum or ask a guide if you prefer.

Find a topic or challenge in this life that you want to work on. We choose here to highlight physical pain in the back. Let's say that at the age of 30 you get a lot of back pain. You go to the doctor but are told that everything looks fine. Nor is there anything in this life that you know of that has happened. Then there is a possibility that this is the consequence of something that happened in a previous life. Here you can investigate by asking and feeling:

- Did this back problem occur in a past life? (Yes)
- Ask to receive information from that life and event. Maybe you get an image, a country or a feeling? Here it is different what people experience depending on how they are used to receiving information. There is no right or wrong.
- If you pick something up, trust that what you pick up is something from that life. Sometimes it can feel like we are

fantasizing but let it be like that at first. The more you trust this, the more you will receive.

- See if you can find the originating event that caused the back problem.
- Go into any feelings that come up and face them. You can also focus on the back or where the pain is.
- If there are strong or traumatic images or feelings, you can take a little at a time.
- When you get the information, ask for help to heal and heal this cell memory and transform the energy.
- In this way, we can access things that affect us from past lives in a fairly simple but powerful way.

If you have difficulty getting up images or memories, feel free to use the pendulum and ask yourself until you have a reasonably clear picture of what happened.

Example:
- Was my back problem created in a past life? (Yes)
- Was I a man in that life? (Yes)
- Was I sick? (No)
- Did I miss something? (Yes)
- Was it an accident? (No)
- Did someone hurt me? (Yes)
- Was it in a fight? (No)
- Was it in war? (Yes)
- Did I die from the injury? (No)
- Was I badly hurt? (Yes)

- Was I paralyzed? (Yes)
- How old was I? (further ask about age)
- Allow any feelings, thoughts and memories to surface.
- Ask your higher self or your guides for help to heal and release this cellular memory and to transform the energy associated with the event. Feel free to focus on the back where the pain is and imagine it healing.

Past Life & Relationships

You can also work with relationships linked to past lives. Here you do in much the same way, only that the questions are directed towards a particular relationship you choose. Let's say you are in a strong soul relationship or with your Twin Flame. Perhaps you have recurring difficulties, patterns or quarrels and feel that you are not progressing. We say that in your relationship you have a great need to step in and protect your partner, perhaps more than your partner appreciates. You argue about this, and you feel like you just want to help while your partner feels supervised. You have difficulty understanding where the behavior comes from. Then you can look to see if this is a pattern you carry with you from a previous life.

In that case, you can investigate by asking questions about past lives between you. Feel free or use a pendulum until you find out what it's coming from. Please ask to receive the original event of what is happening.

It might look like this:

- Was this pattern created in a past life? (Yes)
- Was I a man in that life? (Yes)
- Was my partner a woman? (Yes)
- Have we lived multiple lives with these challenges? (Yes) Often we have had recurring karmic patterns that we work to resolve.
- Did something happen that created this overprotective behavior in me? (Yes)
- Has my partner experienced something in a past life that made me have to protect? (Yes)
- Did I succeed in protecting her in that life? (No)
- Did she die? (Yes)
- Does this create a fear in me of losing her in the present life? (Yes)
- Experience and go into any feelings that come.
- *"I am asking for help to clear this karma and the emotions connected with that event!"*

We have now found where the behavior comes from and by finding it, we can gain an understanding of why this pattern recurs. Based on that, we can dissolve the energy blockage that has been here. Then it is good to be aware of the behavior when it occurs and to actively break it in everyday life.

When you work with past lives, strong emotions may come up that go along with the information you get, but you don't always feel anything. If you don't feel anything, the feelings may come up at a later time. Sometimes we may have an inner resistance to accessing certain things and you can always ask your higher self or your guides to help you release resistance in the process. But the most important thing is that you give it time. It is enough to bring things out, regardless of whether it happens via the pendulum or through your intuition. The rest will fall into place.

Think of your healing journey as a puzzle where you lay one piece at a time. It can be difficult to see the whole picture, but eventually the puzzle is complete, and you see the whole clearly.

Karmic Patterns

The law of karma is one of the universal laws and it means that the energy we send out or are in comes back to us in some form. Simply put, we can say that positive energy creates positivity and negative energy creates negativity. If we are in and sending out love, this love can do nothing but come back to us. If we are in and sending out fear, we create more of that energy in our life. This does not mean that we should go around being positive all the time but rather that we should make choices and act out of love and our truth instead of fear.

The law of karma is not a law aimed at punishing anyone but is objective in itself. However, the law means that all people have their own responsibility and free will, and depending on what we choose to do with this, it will create different types of consequences.

Karma patterns are karmic patterns that we created over several lifetimes and that can be challenging to break. It can be a pattern we created linked to a certain person but also a more general pattern that we created over a long period of time.

It is common that we meet at least one person in life with whom we share strong karmic patterns. It could be a parent, a partner, close friend, etc. Common to these relationships are elements of advantage/disadvantage and some form of power play.

The relationship can contain everything from unhealthy behaviors to highly dysfunctional elements. Many people find it difficult to get out of these relationships, even though there is a clear problem. It is rooted in the recognition and attraction that is often found energetically. We are often drawn to what is familiar to us.

Common karmic patterns that recur in old souls are various forms of codependency. One simply chooses to stay in relationships because of dependency patterns created in the past. This can sit deep within us, and it is important that we become aware of different things we fall back into such as relationship patterns and how we are towards ourselves and others.

An example of a general karmic pattern is that we constantly have difficulty standing up for ourselves. We may have many lives behind us where we have struggled with this theme in different ways and in different constellations. Now it comes up in this life for you to have the opportunity to finally let it go. You will then end up in situations where you are forced to stand up for yourself and when you have learned that task or "lesson" the karma you are carrying will be released.

To work with karmic patterns, you can work by looking at patterns that repeat themselves over and over in your life, especially in relationships. You can also work in a similar way as in the previous exercise where you ask questions.

Chapter 18

DNA, FAMILY LINES AND
THE COLLECTIVE

Not only that we carry with us challenges from childhood and past lives. We inherit the trauma of our previous generations, which means we can experience feelings of a trauma that our mother or grandmother experienced. A trauma can pass through as many as 10 generations before it begins to be neutralized energetically. It is a complex process but also unique in its own way.

When we experience trauma, changes are created in our DNA and our cells - our cells start to behave differently. One reason why trauma is passed on from generation to generation is to give them another chance to heal. If the person who experiences a trauma is unable to face and process the trauma, then it is passed on to the next generation so that person will have the opportunity to process and resolve the trauma. Think of cancer or back problems that are passed down from generation to generation. The same applies with our emotions. If your mother has had PTSD but hasn't been helped to deal with it, chances are you will experience the same kind of feelings. This is because the energy is passed on via DNA and cells, but also because you as a child absorb and take in your mother's energy, thus also her unprocessed emotions and trauma. Highly sensitive people absorb energies to an even greater degree than people who are less sensitive.

We can therefore experience strong emotions and fears that are not even ours to begin with. How is it then that some traumas are passed on and others are not? The most decisive factor that we have seen lies in whether people have talked about what happened or whether it has been hushed up. Let's say your grandmother has been exposed to a trauma where she lost a child. Because of the times she lived in and because of a lack of support from those around her, she was unable to process the incident, but put the lid on it. She took strong medications and sedatives for a long time, and she never talked about what happened.

As we have learned by now, strong emotions need to be expressed and when they are not allowed to do so, they have to go somewhere, namely into the body. The energy from the trauma thus remains in the body and when your grandmother has a child, this energy is passed on to the daughter. The daughter is probably unaware of this but experiences strong fears and anxieties arising from the incident. She then has a child herself and that child is you! You too get this energy connected to the trauma and in this way, we can bring with us greater blockages and limitations that originate far back in time. In this way, we also inherit our parents' diseases such as asthma and arthritis. We are also at greater risk of getting breast cancer if our mother had it.

By working with these blockages, the energy that is tied to the trauma is released and you prevent it from being passed on to future generations. If you already have children, you can still work on this because all the healing you do for yourself affects your children and your family in a positive way. The energy changes within you and thus in the relationship with your children.

To examine what we may carry with us from previous generations, it is valuable to look at what your greatest fears are. We all have our great basic fears and some of them we may have created in this life, but there is a probability that you got them already as a fetus in your mother's womb. It is especially important to look at the fears that you do not understand or know where they come from, i.e. fears that you cannot find an explanation for.

Ask yourself questions such as:

- If everything around me was destroyed - what is my greatest fear?
- What is my biggest and deepest fear in life? Maybe it's not being loved, being abandoned, losing everyone you have around you or dying. After you locate one or a few major fears, you can look to see if there is any traumatic event in the past that could be behind it.

How can we heal the trauma in the family line?

Step one in all healing work is about creating an awareness, exploring and picking up your curiosity. As soon as we become aware of the underlying wounds and traumas that exist, a healing process begins, and the trauma no longer has the same power over us. In addition, you are showing the Universe that you are ready to heal and move forward in that area.

Examine patterns in the family. Has your mother or father had a big fear? Perhaps there has been a strong fear in the family of not making it financially. Maybe you know that mom was involved in something big when she was younger that affected her.

Work a lot with healing in your three lower chakras. Here the Root Chakra is central because it is connected with our family, kindred and our roots. It is the first chakra that is programmed and developed within us in the mother's womb. Here we carry a lot of what we got from mother, her feelings and unprocessed events.

You can also ask for help from your higher guide team in the form of Archangels and Ascended Masters. Ask them for help in healing the traumas and fears back in the family line and in clearing energy from trauma at the cellular level. Feel free to sit down for a moment and focus on this exercise. See if any feelings, memories or other things come up that can serve as clues.

Another exercise for Healing
Let's say you have a deep fear of giving birth. You don't know why because you haven't had children and therefore have no experience of it yourself. Here you can ask if this fear comes from the family.

You can ask the following:
- Does the fear come from my family? (Yes)
- From dad's side? (No)
- From the mother's side? (Yes)
- How many generations back was this fear created? (1? 2? 3? 4? Yes) So it was created four generations back.
- Did something happen in that life that caused this fear? (Yes)
- Did the woman miscarry? (No)
- Did something happen at birth? (Yes)
- Did the baby die at birth? (Yes)
- Did this create a trauma for the woman? (Yes)
- Did she get help to process this? (No)
- Did she repress the incident? (Yes)

- Ask to clear: *"I ask for help to heal this cellular memory, to clear and heal these feelings in the entire family line until today. I am asking for healing for this event on a cellular level. Help me restore my DNA completely!"*

The energy from the Collective

The earth we live on has in itself a high and fine energy frequency. We don't want to change that energy, and it's not something we need to heal either. When we in Spirituality speak of ascension and healing for the collective, we are not referring to the planet in its pure form but our collective consciousness. Our collective consciousness is the stream of energy that is constantly around us, like a cloud of information and experience. The collective consciousness consists of all the knowledge and information we carry as humans here on earth. Together, this flow of information forms what we call Collective Consciousness. Simplistically, you can say that the collective consciousness creates the reality we have around us. We know what we can do, and we know what we can't do. But as we bring new experiences into this consciousness it expands, and we raise the general frequency on Earth (or in the collective consciousness).

Based on this, we always help to heal the collective consciousness when we work with healing within ourselves. Everything we do affects people around us, both positive and negative events.

We are constantly affected by energies that are around us and if you are highly sensitive, you pick up energies and emotions from your surroundings but also from the collective. You feel the pain of people's experiences in the world.

Throughout time, society has had different types of norms or so-called templates, which are templates for how we should live and be. These templates create strong energies that we feel, and it is often difficult to break away from these common beliefs that are around us. It can be ideas about how a man or woman should be. We are constantly taking in these energies and incorporating them into our energy system.

Sometimes we can also sense when something terrible has happened in a particular place. Some people feel strong negative emotions and sadness when they visit places where the Second World War took place. Of course, we can all be depressed by being in a place where people have had to put their lives on the line, but many highly sensitive people pick up on these feelings and take them in as their own. Major events that took place in history are constantly present around us and we take it in to varying degrees. We can even see it as Country karma, where different parts of the world struggle with a heavy and low vibration.

When we have reached a certain point in our spiritual journey, it is common for us to open up even more to the collective flow and this can sometimes make it difficult for us to be out among people. Here it is valuable to learn to distinguish one's own energy from that of others, so that we notice if we start to pick up a lot of weight from the environment. With training and awareness, we can discern this, which makes it easier for us. Then we know when we are in our own feelings or carrying around others'.

To heal for the Collective

In order to work with the collective, it is positive if you can capture a certain feeling or condition you carry. Maybe you've been out for a day on the town and when you get home you experience strong feelings of anger and frustration. You don't know why and actually you've had a nice day. Nor has anything in particular happened that you are angry about. But the anger is there and creates a pressure on the chest.

We can also become aware of if we experience very strong emotions in everyday life that we cannot connect to any particular event here and now. These could be old feelings within you coming up, but they could also be collective feelings you pick up. If we follow the media and are fed information about violent crimes or other serious matters, we can pick up collective emotions in the form of anger, frustration or general fear.

To work on healing collective emotions, we recommend that you ask questions and then clear the current energy. So, use your pure intuition or a pendulum and ask questions to find out more about what you are carrying.

If you feel a lot of frustration, you can ask:

- Is this my anger I feel (No)
- Are they feelings from the collective? (Yes) That can be enough. You can ask more questions, but you can otherwise choose to clear this energy.
- Ask your higher self or your guides for help clearing this energy. For example: *"I ask my highest guides for help to clear and lift away all the frustration I have picked up from the collective. Clear*

all chakras, emotional, mental and energetic. Clear all energy I carry

that is not mine! Thanks!"

Chapter 19

In this part of the book, we will delve into the topic of Trauma, and we will also go into more detail about what is called Soul Fragmentation.

What is a Trauma?

The term Trauma is something we have been in contact with a lot during our work, both in terms of ourselves but also in the clients we work with. In order to heal a trauma, we need to understand which mechanisms are involved when we experience a trauma. There are no definite things or events that cause trauma, but it is a subjective event in the person who experiences it. This means that one person can be part of an abuse, without being traumatized, while another person can create a large and deep trauma within themselves.

A trauma is an event where we feel that we are unable to handle, process and process what is happening. It becomes overwhelming and, in many cases, our internal defense mechanisms step in and help us deal with the emotions that arise, in order to cope. A defense can be that we shut down and lose contact with what is happening. This is not something we do consciously, but it is our inner self trying to protect us from overwhelming pain.

A trauma often affects us mentally, emotionally and energetically. Within psychology and behavioral science, a lot of focus is often placed on our thoughts and feelings when it comes to trauma and what happens inside us. We want to highlight that the energy part is

218

at least as important and we need to look at what is happening to us in terms of energy. When we experience a trauma, it always affects our energy in a tangible way. It creates a strong imbalance within us and to restore this imbalance we need to heal the trauma in terms of energy.

Depending on what we are involved with, it can affect one or more of our chakras. Imagine that you are involved in a car accident where the car you are driving runs off the road, veers off the side of the road and hits a tree. During this short time, you have time to think that you are going to die, you feel strong fear and have difficulty breathing. You manage but after the accident you are in shock. You have difficulty getting down in pulse and you feel a constant sense of panic and fear in the coming days. This event could affect you in the following ways:

Mentally: You create recurring thoughts that you will die.
Emotionally: You constantly feel a strong fear and a lot of discomfort inside.
Energy-wise: Your Root Chakra is strongly affected and ends up in great imbalance, this because the chakra is connected with our survival and safety.

If we only work with our thoughts, we still carry the energy connected with the trauma within us. We have been in contact with many people who have tried to process and heal trauma by changing thought processes alone. But it is often difficult, because we are deep and complex energy beings. Sometimes it can be enough to work with mental changes and to work with emotional management. But if you are an old soul, you most likely need to delve into and understand the energetic part. You don't need to understand everything, but it is valuable to know that your energy is being affected. When we are involved in a trauma, the chakra associated with that particular area of life is often affected. Of course, several chakras can be affected when you are involved in something, but it can be good to start somewhere.

Below are examples of how each chakra can be affected by trauma.

The Root Chakra

Here we usually see events connected with pure survival, safety and security. It could be an accident, or we feel very unsafe at home due to violence or major conflicts. There can also be events where we are exposed to something by another person and where we feel that we cannot protect ourselves.

The Sacral Chakra

Trauma can affect our Sacral Chakra when we experience events connected to our sexuality, our emotions, intimacy and creativity. An example could be experiences of sexual abuse or some form of sexual harassment. Being bullied or subjected to great abuse as a child can also settle strongly in the Sacral Chakra. The chakra is also associated with trauma that raises a lot of guilt.

The Solar Plexus Chakra

This chakra is greatly affected by the trauma associated with our personality, self-worth and power. The energy can become unbalanced here if we become very vulnerable because of our personality or if as children we feel that we have no value. It could also be that you feel deep shame in connection with an event.

The Heart Chakra

The heart chakra represents our deep and close relationships, our love for ourselves, trust and our sense of belonging. The traumas that affect this chakra are events where we experience a great betrayal by a person or when we are exposed to something by someone who is very close to us. An example is if we have a narcissistic parent who treats us badly as a child.

The Throat Chakra

This chakra is affected by trauma where we are heavily silenced, for example by a parent or someone close to us. It may be that we are not allowed to be ourselves or that we are strongly questioned for something we say. The chakra can also take a lot of damage if we live for a long time in some form of lie where we are not true to ourselves.

The Third Eye

The third eye is affected by events where we are deprived of the opportunity to live according to our own vision or truth. It could be that we grow up in a family with very strong beliefs, are part of a sect or some other context where we are more or less forced to give up our own inner convictions.

The Crown Chakra

Here we have the trauma connected with our thoughts, how we see, believe and think about things. Here is also our perception of ourselves and other people. This chakra is greatly affected by events where we feel that we are losing control of ourselves or our existence. It can also be shown by the fact that we feel that we lose contact with ourselves or where we experience strong stress.

Common Signs of Unprocessed Trauma

When we have unprocessed trauma in our body, it affects us in many different ways. In some cases, it may be difficult to see or feel that we are carrying an unprocessed trauma, while in other cases it is more evident. If we experienced something traumatic as young children, we don't always remember the event itself, especially if it happened at a very early age.

Sometimes we know something has happened but not quite what. We humans are good at repressing things we've been through to avoid internal pain and discomfort. The points below show how an unprocessed trauma can manifest itself in us:

- Strong feelings of anxiety in everyday life, without us knowing where it comes from
- Great difficulty sleeping for a long time
- Different forms of compulsion or behaviors where we escape from strong emotions
- Great difficulty in experiencing our emotions, feeling of exclusion
- Great difficulty being close to other people intimately or in other ways
- Feelings of disaster or recurring thoughts of disaster
- Strong feelings of insecurity

- Excessively strong emotions in everyday life that affect us negatively
- Difficult to remember large parts of one's childhood
- Sexually shut down
- Exalted sexuality
- Addiction or various types of strong addictions
- Feelings of not wanting to live
- Excessively strong control needs where we want to control ourselves or others

There may of course be other indications that you are carrying a trauma, and the nuances may differ in what we experience. But if it is the case that you have one or more of these points that recur, you can ask yourself if something happened that may have created a trauma within you. Maybe you know with you that you have been through difficult things during your life. Remember that it is not the event itself that determines whether it is a trauma, but how you experience it.

In our work, we have noticed that those who have experienced major trauma in their upbringing often speak quite favorably or neutrally about their upbringing, while those who have had a calmer life can speak very negatively about their upbringing. Our conclusion about that is that the people who carry great trauma embellish what happened or they have learned to create distance from it - so much distance that they no longer know about what happened. We all have a part within us that wants to protect, both ourselves and our parents. But here it is important that you are honest with yourself in order to be able to access and heal your inner self.

Dealing with strong Emotions & Trauma

When it comes to any form of trauma management, it is important to proceed carefully. If we have been through trauma or carry very strong emotions, we can be overwhelmed by the emotions that come up and this can create fear and resistance. If you have strong fear, think about and do the following:

- Be aware of emotions and their true nature! Emotions are never really dangerous in themselves, but it is the resistance and fear of the emotions that we do everything to avoid. Emotions in their pure form are just energy and when we feel an emotion in our body, it is energy impulses that go through our body. What determines whether a feeling is unpleasant or pleasant is the frequency at which the feeling vibrates. The lower the frequency, the more discomfort we experience as a rule. Think of it as low-vibrational energy passing through your body. Emotions such as guilt, shame, anger and sadness vibrate at a low frequency and therefore we do everything we can to avoid feeling these emotions. But the more we can work our way through these, the more we can experience high emotions such as peace, harmony and joy. By being aware that it is energy that passes through the body, it can make it easier and as said, no feeling is really dangerous even if it can be unpleasant in the moment.

- If you feel that your emotions are becoming overwhelming, take it a little at a time. Feel the feeling when it comes and then stop. Then repeat the same process at a later time. You never need to stress in these processes but try not to run away from what you need to face. Be humble and listen to your needs.

- If you feel you need support and help, you can do these processes partly on your own and partly with a therapist or healer who can help you through it. We all have the ability to heal ourselves on all levels, but sometimes we may need a little support and help along the way.

- Ask guides and archangels for help in dealing with your pain! You can also ask the angels to take your pain and free you as much as possible. Send out your intention and say what you want help with and then have trust.

Exercises for working with a Trauma

You can work with trauma in several different ways. Here we will cover two different exercises that you can work on. When it comes to all the healing and all the exercises we highlight in this book, it basically comes down to the same thing; we want to lift up and raise awareness of the energy and the feeling that is locked somewhere inside us. By doing so, we heal from the ground up. This means that we can heal things in an infinite number of ways and that no way is really wrong. Blockages are always created by avoiding or repressing the feelings and thoughts that arise in a situation. By lifting up these thoughts and feelings and the energy, we release the blockage and begin to heal. As we mentioned earlier, traumatic events affect our thoughts, our emotions and our chakras. By extension, it can also affect our physical body, our cells and our organs because everything is a whole and belongs together.

Start by looking at whether there is a trauma or something that you know is affecting you. We take an example that deals with childhood. Let's say that in your childhood you had an unstable father who could get very angry. At one point it went so far that he really scared you and you even got physical blows from him. This came as a shock to you, and you had a hard time dealing with the experience. You felt strong feelings of shame and fear. This happened when you were around 12 years old. Today you remember the event rather vaguely. You remember it happening, but it doesn't evoke any emotion in you when you think about it. But every time you are close to your father, you experience resistance and discomfort. In your relationship with your partner, you are easily startled, and you feel shame as soon as he points out the smallest thing you do, even if it's just taking out the dishwasher in a different way. It may seem strange that such an act would still affect you, and besides, it was so long ago that it happened. But for a child of that age, it can create enormous fear and if it becomes too difficult to handle, there is a great risk that you shut down the feelings that arose in the situation. They then remain there within you, vibrating, as a reminder of something that is not quite resolved. Our body always strives for balance, and it shows us where we are out of balance through fear, pain, discomfort and so on.

To work with this, you can use a pendulum and ask questions or feel in freely with intuition.

Exercise:

- Sit comfortably and set an intention from your heart to heal and to free yourself from this past event. By setting that intention, you have already started the process.

- First, ask yourself questions and start investigating the incident. You can ask things like: What do I remember from the event? What emotions did I experience? How did I handle this? Can I recognize these feelings in my life now as an adult? When will they arrive? Dare to look deeper into this and see what happens. Maybe you get in touch with emotions connected to the situation or you don't.

- Allow yourself to just meet what comes. It can be thoughts and feelings.

- Feel free to ask the question about what happened that affected one of your chakras and try to pay attention to which chakra it is by feeling in your body. It may be that you feel a sensation around the heart or further down in the stomach. You may just know which chakra it affected. Trust what you get or feel. You can also use a pendulum and ask if you want.

- When you have a little more clarity on what happened and where it sits - ask your highest guidance team and your higher self to heal this within you.

- For example: *"I am asking my higher self and my highest guide team to help me heal blockages from this event. Help me heal thoughts, feelings, energetically and on a cellular level. I free myself from what happened and allow myself to feel the emotions that need to come up to heal."*

Sometimes feelings related to the event surface a few days or weeks later. If it is something that has been hidden inside you for a long time, it may take some time before you release and heal it. If you feel that nothing is happening, wait a few days and then do the same exercise again. We may have to work over and over again with things that we have carried for a long time. The greater the pain we experienced, the more resistance we may have created. Here we need to be patient and trust our soul to help us let it go.

You can also choose to do the same exercise if you experience strong emotions linked to a certain stressful event or trauma. If it is the case that you have very strong feelings, it may be difficult to do exactly the steps that we mentioned in the exercise above. If you experience a lot of discomfort, stress or pain, you can just sit down and try to face what comes up. Try to stay in the feelings that come up, whatever comes up - at least for a little while. When you feel it starting to calm down, you can ask questions about what you are feeling. Ask yourself where the feelings come from, if you recognize them from before and where in the body they are. Use your pendulum or intuition to get the answers. If you try several times and find that it becomes too overwhelming, it can be positive to seek the help of a good healer or therapist.

Dealing with Emotional Dissociation

In the same way that we can have strong emotions that come to the surface after difficult events, we can also experience the opposite, that we do not have access to our emotions. When we experience something in our environment that we cannot take in and process at the time, our body has a special defense mechanism that causes us to push the feeling away, into the subconscious. This means that we don't have to face and deal with the feeling in the moment, but the problem is that the feeling and its energy still remain within us in our subconscious - and affect us throughout life. This is also called dissociation and sometimes we can have so much dissociated emotions that we don't even know we have them. Often much of this pattern already happens in early childhood, which also means that we may not remember the event itself.

Here it is important to start finding a way to bring up these feelings so that healing can take place. If you find it very difficult to feel anger or sadness, so difficult that you cannot get in touch with them, then there is a high probability that there are feelings you have closed down. So, if you feel closed off or have difficulty getting in touch with your feelings, you can do the following:

- Take a moment every day where you are JUST present in your body. Feel free to sit or lie down and just let go of all demands and musts. Just be present in your body and observe how it feels. Often, when we have difficulty being in touch with our inner emotional life, we have shifted our focus up to our head and our thoughts. This means that we are in the thought a lot and many times we can even find it difficult to be in the body. It has become a kind of escape from ourselves. In this exercise we get an opportunity to get to know our body again, to resume the contact we lost with the body. So, observe your body. How does it feel? Can you feel any sensation and if so, what? Is there discomfort anywhere? Does it tingle? Just focus all the time where you feel any sensation.

- When we have difficulty getting in touch with our emotions, we also have difficulty being grounded, this because we fled from our body and our emotions for a long time. When we escape from the body and are very much in our thoughts, we become very ungrounded. So, find a way to ground yourself, for example, be in nature or take long, deep breaths. By becoming more grounded, you get more in touch with both yourself and Mother Earth. That in itself helps you heal and absorb healing energy from the earth.

- Do things that are out of your comfort zone. Often, we do the same or similar things and activities during the day, which in itself does not have to be wrong. But what often happens is that we do what we are safe with and then we also don't face new types of challenges and feelings within us. So, a tip here to do something that you are not comfortable with because it is a good way to bring up emotions in the body, both positive emotions and negative ones. It's hard to do something that we're not used to or something where we really need to go outside the safe space without experiencing something. So do things that evoke emotional reactions within you and when those feelings come, meet them and give appreciation for them coming and for experiencing them. Remember that all emotions are basically positive because they show us something and carry information.

- You can also try to evoke certain feelings yourself by spending a moment in which you bring yourself back to a certain event or memory. Think of something that evoked a certain feeling within you and spend some time and energy entering that state. Once you get to it, whether you feel it strongly or just slightly, observe your body and face what comes. Our body is never really turned off, but it always continues to talk to us, but we may need to find our way back to and start listening to it.

- Do something in a conversation with someone that you wouldn't normally do! For example, if you are always the one listening, try taking up a little more space. If you are compliant, try setting a clear boundary. If you find it difficult to express your opinions, express them in a way that feels good to you. This is also a way of getting in touch with things within us that we carry but that we have lost.

Soul Fragmentation (Soul Loss)

We have previously noted that our energy and chakras are affected by traumatic events. Our body is strong, and it is made to cope with a lot. If we look back at how we humans have lived here on earth, we understand that our body is designed to be able to experience and receive a lot of pain, both physically and on the emotional level. But sometimes it gets completely overwhelming! When we are involved in really big and traumatic events, it can lead to soul fragmentation. This is a form of spiritual defense mechanism, and it means that the soul expels part of our soul energy from the body in case of trauma. It may sound strange, but it is the soul's way of protecting us from extreme pain or death. Examples of when this can happen are when we are involved in torture, sexual abuse, severe accidents or war.

The more soul energy we have in the body, the more sensitive we are and the more pain we can feel. By expelling a fragment of the soul, out of our body, the pain becomes less in the moment. So, in the moment it is something positive, but the problem is that this creates some difficulties for us in the long term. We might get over the situation and move on with our lives. This soul energy that we pushed away causes a part of us to be lacking energetically. When we have soul fragmentation, we may experience feelings of confusion or not really having access to our whole selves. It is as if we are missing something within us. In order to feel whole again, we need to bring this energy back into our energy system and into our body. We need to reintegrate spiritual aspects so that we have access to our whole selves and all our energy. It is relatively common for us to carry this blockage from past lives with us. We may have experienced painful things in past lives that created this form of spiritual dissociation.

To heal Soul Fragmentation, we need to work with integration. We need to bring the missing energy back into the rest of our energy system again. Imagine that you are like a puzzle with a hundred assembled pieces and that one piece is missing. This blockage will primarily affect you in the area that is connected with what you experienced at the original event. So, if you were abused in a previous life, you may find that you don't really have access to your sexual energy completely in this life. You work and work to find balance, but it doesn't quite work out.

By looking at what we have been through or at least getting a buzz about it, we begin the process of bringing all energy back into our energy system. We allow all energy to be there as a part of us. Our puzzle is complete!

To heal soul fragmentation, we can work on asking questions and then go more into healing and integration. Start by thinking about whether you have any of the following challenges within you:

- Strong sense of fragmentation, that you feel torn inside
- A strong feeling that you are stuck
- A strong feeling or experience that you are not in touch with certain parts within you
- Withdrawal in a specific area, such as sexuality or spirituality
- Great difficulty in getting in touch with your inner self and your emotions

Look at whether you have been through something that was very traumatic for you in this life or past lives. If you are not sure, you can ask questions. Use your pure intuition or your pendulum.

- Do I have any soul fragmentation affecting me? (Yes)
- Does it come from this life? (No)
- Past life? (Yes)
- Was I a woman in that life? (Yes)
- Was I exposed to something traumatic? (Yes)
- Was I beaten? (No)
- Was I sexually assaulted? (Yes)
- You can now choose to ask more questions or work on healing for what happened. Set a clear intention that you want to heal this soul fragmentation. The clearer and the more power the better. When we really want something from the heart, it is more powerful.

- For example, you can express: *"I now choose to heal completely, from all forms of soul fragmentation connected with this past life. I choose to reintegrate this soul energy into my energy system and into my body. I am asking my higher guide team to help me heal this at the cellular level."*
- Feel free to sit for a while afterwards and allow this process to happen. It may be that you bring up feelings or thoughts connected with the event, but this does not always happen. Allow it to be just as it is and trust that it will heal. Feelings can arise even afterwards.
- You may have to work on this subject a few times, but eventually this will begin to dissolve, and your energy will become more and more complete, more and more integrated with you.

Chapter 20

PHYSICAL PAIN IN THE BODY

In the following part, we delve into the subject of physical pain, something that we have probably all struggled with in some way in our lives. The purpose is not to address all the different forms of pain conditions we can experience, but to open up a new way of looking at the pain we carry.

What is physical pain from a Spiritual Perspective?

In our opinion, all pain has an underlying cause, and all pain can be cured. But it can take time and it often requires a lot of inner work and patience. All pain is individual and depending on your circumstances and what you have been through, healing can take place and look different. Sometimes we resolve the pain in this life and sometimes this healing process can follow us into the next life. We can also carry with us pain from previous incarnations, which sometimes makes it difficult for us to understand where the pain comes from. If as children we are born with major physical difficulties, health problems and chronic ailments, it may be that we carry with us things from previous lives that we are meant to deal with here and now. This does not mean that it is always so, but we have seen many such connections in our work.

We imagine that you were a soldier in a previous life and that you died out on a battlefield from a stab wound in the back. It all happened very quickly, and you were in shock. You died just a few minutes later without having time to take in and process what happened. You were young and about to turn 20 when it happened. In your current life, you are fine during your teenage years, but when you turn 20, you suddenly have back pain. This pain is right in the middle of your spine, and you don't understand where it's coming from. You haven't been exercising incorrectly or experienced anything else that could have caused this pain. You see several doctors, but no one can find any defect or damage connected to your back. This may sound far-fetched, but it is not at all unusual for us to re-experience trauma and physical pain in this life, which actually has its origin in past lives. What happens is that a cellular memory can be activated when we reach the same age or when we are involved in something that triggers and activates this energy within us.

Physical pain occurs when we experience something that we cannot handle or resolve emotionally. So, if you burn yourself on a hot stove top, you will most likely not be able to resolve this in your emotions and you will then experience physical pain. However, there are people who through spirituality, thoughts and by putting themselves in a different state of consciousness can avoid feeling pain. You have probably seen people walking barefoot over hot coals or lying on a mat of nails. These are such examples. Stove burn is a difficult event to work with because it happens so quickly. But when it comes to other areas of life and our overall health, we always get an opportunity to process emotions before it manifests itself in the form of illness and pain.

When we carry heavy or unprocessed emotions for a long time without dealing with them, it creates problems. The emotions themselves have a very low frequency and when they are not allowed to be expressed, we build up a layer of unprocessed emotions within us. Our body always strives for balance and the pain is a way of showing us that something inside us is not quite right. It simply becomes too much for our body to handle. Emotions are pure energy and energy can never be destroyed; it can only be changed. So, the emotions we carry need to go somewhere and in this case they come out in the form of pain. This is how most diseases are structured and you can see special emotional blockages for different types of disease states.

- Rheumatism is often long-term anger that we have turned inward against ourselves.
- Pain in the shoulders and neck often means that we have taken on too much responsibility for others in life, often already in childhood.
- Stiffness in muscles and joints can be a result of experiencing a lot of fear and stress for a long time.
- Pain in the throat can be rooted in a subdued expression.
- Problems with intestines and digestion are often a consequence of unprocessed emotions and low self-esteem.

Hans has previously published the book "Messages for the Soul" where he collected his experiences and his knowledge about this particular subject, after having worked actively with clients for over 20 years. There he highlights connections between specific disease states and what may lie behind them in a purely spiritual sense.

Despite the fact that emotions are a large part of us humans, there is a tendency to diminish its existence, not least in society as a whole. There is more focus on our physical body and emotions are often seen as a weakness. As children, we are often helped to deal with a wound or a physical injury but not our emotions. This means that we also do not learn to meet and deal with them within us in a constructive way.

So, an important part in healing pain is about looking at what is behind the pain in the form of emotions. When you solve the problem on an emotional level, you also solve the physical pain. This is because the body then no longer has any need to physically express what you carry inside you.

In many parts of the world, especially where people live close to nature, it is common for people to learn to deal with emotions as part of life. The spirituality created in the West in recent decades has placed a lot of focus on thought processes such as thinking correctly and positively. There is also often a lot of focus on eating right and exercising right. All of this in itself is positive, but sometimes we may miss the most important part – dealing with and understanding our emotions. Many of us can deal with emotions in everyday life such as irritation, frustration or a little general stress. But when it comes to meeting, understanding and dealing with our deepest feelings and our inner self, we often have no idea how to do it. We therefore avoid this as far as we can, because we haven't actually been taught how to deal with it. Today, it is also common to take medication for anxiety and depression, which can lead to suppressing one's feelings, rather than highlighting them and thus healing.

There are many stories around the world of people who have been sick, even dying, but who through deep transformation and healing have been completely restored. Nothing is impossible to heal but it can take time, depending on how long we have carried the pain. It may also be that we suppress our pain and that it then disappears temporarily. But what happens is that it often comes back in a different form, because the emotional cause has not been addressed and healed. All the pain we carry is a messenger and it wants to show us something. It shows us where we took on too much responsibility, where we broke down in self-love, how we dealt with our fears and also what we got from our parents through our genetic inheritance.

We cannot emphasize enough how extremely important it is here not to blame yourself. Guilt holds us back and there is no reason to go into guilt. We need to look at what is there and then face ourselves with extra courage and love. One of the biggest reasons we create pain in the first place is a lack of self-love. All old souls we have met, including ourselves, have had challenges with pain of some kind. Everyone has their own and the more sensitivity we develop here on earth, the tougher it can be to handle all emotions. In addition to that, we may have had a dysfunctional upbringing where we received a variety of heavy and traumatic things.

Healing Physical Pain

Healing pain means diving deep inside and being curious about yourself. We need to create awareness around our body and what it wants to say to us. So, the first step is always to create an awareness of the pain we carry and then ask questions. For example, if you have muscle aches, you can ask yourself the following questions:

- How long have I had this pain?
- Did something painful or difficult happen in my life in connection with the onset of the pain? Not sure you remember

but just look at what pops up. Consider it more of an inquiry than a must-know.

- What is behind the pain? It can be feelings of worry, sadness, anger, guilt or other. Trust what comes to you.
- Is there anyone in my family who has similar pain, for example mother, grandmother or another person?
- Do I myself have any thoughts or ideas about why the pain occurred?

Feel free to spend some time asking questions and you can take other questions or add questions to get more answers. See if you can connect the pain with one of your seven chakras.

A key to balancing and healing our physical body is to really take the time to get to know it. For example, do you know what your body feels good about and what it doesn't feel good about? Do you know which emotions you are in touch with and which emotions you are not in touch with at all? Are there feelings you have never been in touch with at all? If we grew up in a family where we had to repress all the anger we carried, it may be precisely that anger that creates health problems for us. Anger is a powerful and strong energy. When we are not allowed to express it, it often settles as a physical imbalance sooner or later. A lot of stress during growing up often leads to problems with the neck, shoulders, stiffness and pain in muscles and joints. You may have heard of the expression "frozen with horror". When we live in constant worry, it affects our body tremendously, especially when we don't find a way to express these feelings in everyday life. If we live in a troubled growing up environment, we learn to be on full alert and to take in everything that happens around us. We cannot relax and this tension can eventually set in as chronic stiffness in muscles and joints. If we take on too much responsibility at an early age, we get neck and shoulder problems, because we literally carry too much on our shoulders.

Exercise for Healing

The chart on page 243 shows common reasons why we develop physical pain. As we mentioned earlier – all physical pain has an underlying cause, often an image or feeling we need to see and face within ourselves. By bringing out the underlying feeling, we access that energy, and we immediately begin an inner healing process.

We may have to work with this several times and there may be several different feelings behind a state of pain. This exercise is about finding the cause and getting behind the pain in your physical body. You can feel in freely with your intuition or use a pendulum.

You can ask:
- What feeling is behind my back pain?
- Is there anything in row 1? (No) Row 2? (Yes) Then we know it's something in row two.
- Is there anything in column 1? (Yes)
- Now we know there is something in row 2 column 1.
- Now we can continue to ask more specifically.
- Is it fear of letting go of control? (No)
- Is it the feeling of not being enough? (Yes)
- Okay! Behind your pain is a feeling that you are not good enough.

- Investigate this carefully and see where it comes from. Is it something you brought with you from home? Maybe you needed to be a certain way at home to be loved? Maybe there were high demands on you to perform?
- Then ask your higher self and higher guide team to help you heal this within. Feel free to sit for a while and face the thoughts and feelings that come up. It is also incredibly valuable to work here with a lot of self-love. For example, you can put your hand on your heart while expressing pride in yourself. If you have a hard time feeling it, do it anyway, until it gets easier.

Emotion map – What is behind my pain?

Column	1	2	3
Row 1	Grief from childhood. Grief from past lives. Pain from childhood. Past life pain.	Feeling of failure. Feeling of bitterness Feeling of powerlessness. Feeling of abandonment. Impotence.	Prolonged stress. Prolonged fear. Lack of self-love. Hard on myself. Anger
2	Fear of letting go Feeling of not being enough. Feeling of not being worthy of good things. General Fear.	Feelings of disaster. Past life trauma. Fear of change. Fear for life. Childhood trauma.	Holding myself back. Holding too much inside me. Co-dependency. Self hatred.
3	Judge myself harshly. Don't like myself. Hate my body. See me as weak. Feelings of shame.	Not comfortable in my body. Resistance to emotions. Afraid of my feelings. I feel disconnected. Feelings of guilt.	Was seriously ill in a previous life. Difficult to make my voice heard. Don't see my worth. Fear of moving forward.

You can also choose to continue by asking if there are more things on the chart that are behind your pain. Maybe there are 3-4 things that create pain in the same place in your body.

Feel free to do this exercise once or twice a week and work with the feelings that come up. Work with healing but also with change in your everyday life. If you find that there is a lot of anger inside you, find a way to express your anger. Maybe you can take a moment where you actively focus on everything that makes you angry. Allow yourself to truly experience anger and then ask for help to let it go. Experiencing emotions is never negative in itself, it is when we repress or avoid them that they can create problems.

If you find yourself carrying sadness, look at what the sadness is about. Allow yourself to be vulnerable and to experience the heaviness and pain of life. Sometimes we take on a role where we have to be good and keep ourselves together at all costs. We have seen that many people who constantly struggle, keep everything together and are positive, are often the ones who get sick. If you are an empath, highly sensitive or an old soul, you need to allow yourself to be the vulnerable one. Allow yourself to be cared for and let go of the need to be strong all the time.

If it appears that you are holding yourself back, find a way to express more of yourself and your energy in everyday life. Many people who carry a lot of anxiety and who also struggle with very different physical symptoms, are often people who early on learn to direct their emotions inward. This is because the person does not want to be a nuisance or because you have learned from home that your feelings are not appreciated. When we direct our emotions inward, they remain in our energy body. If we find a way to express the feelings outward, it can help us get them out and thus free ourselves from them. Empaths and highly sensitive people almost always choose to direct their energy inward to make things easier for those around them. This builds up and eventually comes out in the form of pain. So, find different ways to express yourself in life. Express your energy! Many people find that creative exercises or activities facilitate the expression of inner feelings. It is precisely because the person then channels the energy or feeling, perhaps in the form of a painting or in a song text.

Chapter 21

SOUL ARCHETYPES AND BLOCKAGES

We will now look more deeply at soul archetypes. The concept of Archetype has a strong connection with psychology and Carl Jung. Here we choose to highlight archetypes as a Role or as a certain Type of energy we enter during life here on earth.

Depending on what our life looks like and what our life's purpose is, we can have different soul archetypes that dominate and are more prominent. We may also have developed strong archetypes in past lives that are activated at some point in this life. An example of this is when we have children for the first time. Then the archetype The Mother can be activated very powerfully within us and becomes a large part of us and what we do. The same is true if we go into a spiritual awakening and all of a sudden have a strong attraction to spirituality and healing. We're going more into The Healer archetype.

The purpose of this chapter is not to cover all the archetypes that exist as there are an infinite number. One purpose is to give you an understanding of how these archetypes can affect you, depending on whether they are in balance or imbalance. You have now hopefully realized on a deep level that you are an old soul, and this means that you had many, perhaps hundreds of archetypes and roles in your past lives. These archetypes are extremely valuable, as they are part of the knowledge and strengths you have developed over all these lifetimes. They show what roles your soul has been in many times and by becoming aware of this you can open up more to that energy here and now.

Archetypes in themselves are neither positive nor negative, but it is how we use its properties and energy that determines the outcome. An archetype becomes unbalanced when we use its energy to harm ourselves or when we are involved in a major trauma connected with that particular energy. Let's say you had several lives as a Healer where you helped people. In one life you were Native Indian, and you carried a strong healing energy as a shaman. You were proud of yourself, and many appreciated your immense wisdom and the help you provided. But one day something happened that made you lose your composure completely. The village you lived in was attacked by the English and several in the village were killed. You were captured and forced to shut down your spirituality.

In the present life, you are entering a spiritual awakening, and you feel drawn to continue healing. But there are great fears within you. You doubt yourself and you don't dare to take the step and work on healing. The fear and uncertainty take over and just the thought of doing it makes you lose your composure. Because of what happened, you have gone from The Healer archetype to The wounded Healer. In this life, you need to dare to face the pain and fear associated with this archetype and energy, in order to do your life's work and help yourself and others.

An archetype can also become unbalanced if we have strong abilities in a certain area that we abuse or where we harm other people.

Let's look at The Communicator archetype. This archetype has an energy of leadership skills and strong communication skills. People who are writers, leaders or teachers often have this archetype strongly within them. There are powerful communicators who abuse this energy, causing the energy to become unbalanced. An example of this would be a cult leader who has the ability to get people to listen but uses this for a destructive purpose. Another example was Adolf Hitler who was a good communicator but used these qualities in a very negative way.

Working with archetypes is an exploration of oneself and one's qualities here on earth. By becoming aware that you have different archetypes within you, you can begin to discover, see and develop these in a more concrete way. Sometimes it can be difficult to know which are our strongest archetypes, but often we know roughly. We know which things and areas we are very strongly drawn to, and we often have a sense of what we are good at and what our natural talents are. If not, you will discover this more during your spiritual journey and the more you heal within yourself. To heal yourself is to find home within yourself and when we do that, we gain more and more access to all parts of us.

We will now address 9 different soul archetypes that we have seen are quite common for old souls. Often, we have had one or more of these archetypes in past lives and many times in this life as well. To further clarify what an archetype is, you can think of it as an area within you or in life where your energy is extra strong and powerful – a part of you that can help you express yourself or do what you need to do. We also show how each archetype can express itself depending on whether it is in balance or imbalance.

The Healer

The Healer carries the energy of healing. It can apply to healing for oneself but also for other people. This is the classic healer, but we also see this archetype in other helping professions such as doctor, naturopath, medicine man and therapist. When this energy is in balance, we see a person who helps other people on the planet for the better. A classic and very good example of this archetype in balance is Jesus. We are not believers in the classical sense but believe that Jesus was a great healer when he lived on earth. We often use his energy when we work with healing and energy work. When this archetype is out of balance, we can see a person using healing power for their own gain or by manipulating people. It could be a person who has healing abilities but uses it in a harmful way. The opposite of the balanced archetype here is also called, as we mentioned earlier, The wounded Healer.

Keyword
Balance: Healer, helps heal self and others, integrity.
Imbalance: Uses healing to hurt, no boundaries, helps at the expense of own well-being, fear linked with his healing abilities.

The Mother
The Mother carries the energy of nurturing. It is the person who is "everyone's mother" and to whom people come for help and support. This energy is basically very nice and if we use it in a positive way, we can be a great support to people around us, including ourselves. Here it is important to take care of yourself and not take too much responsibility for other people. We really only have responsibility for ourselves and our children until they are of age. If you have a very caring side that constantly shines through, you probably have a lot of this archetype within you. A fine example of this archetype in balance

is Mary Magdalene, Jesus' Twin Flame and other half. Maria Magdalena has a feminine, soft and loving energy. If the energy is unbalanced, we can see it in self-sacrifice and self-effacement, abandoning ourselves to care for others. Here we go more towards The Martyr archetype.

Keyword
Balance: Loving, caring, giving, helpful, clear boundaries.
Imbalance: Martyr, excessive responsibility and sacrifice, burnout.

The Psychic

The Psychic carries the energy and ability to see, pick up and interpret spiritual messages or information from other dimensions. This can happen in different ways and through our different senses. These are people who are mediums and who receive strong messages from angels or guides. If this energy is used in a positive way, that archetype can help many people by channeling and receiving messages. If the archetype is used or expressed in a more unbalanced way, we can see a person using divine information to boost their own ego or oppress other people. There is another archetype called The Magician and these two are very similar. The latter is more about magic and about using magic for different purposes. Many of you may have seen the movie The Lord of the Rings. There we have a clear and good example of The Magician in balanced and more unbalanced form. We have Gandalf who is the good wizard and who uses his magic to help. Then we have Saruman, the evil wizard who uses his magic to harm and create power.

Balance: Channels information and guidance that helps and develops.
Imbalance: Uses mediumistic abilities for manipulation or in a way
that harms self or others.

The Explorer

The Explorer carries the energy of exploration and discovery. A
person with this energy strongly within them wants to discover and
see new things, both within themselves but also out in the world.
There is great curiosity and a strong need to learn, understand and
absorb new knowledge. This archetype is valuable because people
with this energy open up new paths and lead people forward. They
are people who leave the crowd and go their own way, regardless of
what others think or think about it. Without people with this
archetype, we would have no development. Here we see people like
Einstein and Columbus. The unbalanced part here can be that we are
constantly on the run, that we have a hard time grounding ourselves
and that we run away from ourselves and everyday life. It also often
means that we run away from our feelings and what we need to see
and heal within.

Keyword

Balance: Discovers, explores and develops new paths, opportunities.
Imbalance: Volatile, difficult to be grounded and to meet one's inner
self and to settle down.

The Nurturer

The Nurturer carries the energy of nurturing. These are people who have often spent many lives in aid organizations or various forms of nursing professions.

It could be someone who works as a nurse, midwife or similar. This is also where the empath comes in, the one who feels the pain of others and who wants to help everything and everyone. A very fine and loving energy when used in a constructive and balanced way. In its balanced form, we see it as nurturing and the one that devotes a lot of time and energy to helping. The slightly more unbalanced part of the archetype can show itself through co-dependency and that we help others too much, at the expense of our own well-being.

Keyword

Balance: Nurturing and caring towards self and others.
Imbalance: Giving too much to others, lack of boundaries, depleting one's own energy and power.

The Work horse

The Work horse carries the energy of hard work and toil. We see this archetype in people who work on and who are always moving forward. You know that person who is always working and making things go around. This archetype is very positive when balanced because things happen. We move out of stagnation and make things manifest and take shape in the physical. When this energy is out of balance, we can see it in people who burn themselves out over and over again, people who don't know when the limit of hard work has been reached. This archetype is also associated with slavery and working hard for little or no money. If we had one or more past lives as a slave or serf, it can make this archetype very unbalanced or damaged within us. We may then toil hard without seeing or feeling our own worth.

Keyword
Balance: Working efficiently, moving forward, making things happen, creating.
Imbalance: Workaholic, working too hard, slavery, working a lot in relation to what you get in return, physical ill health.

The Rebel

The Rebel carries the energy of reform and liberation. It can be about reforms in society or within ourselves. There is a great need to go one's own way and to do things one's way, unlike the great mass of society. Many who had this archetype strongly in previous lives have created great changes in society, but many have also had bad luck, precisely because they got in the way. In today's Western world, there are fairly large opportunities to think and think freely compared to how it looked a hundred years ago. The rebel archetype creates things in their own unique way and often has difficulty taking orders from others or following authority.

Keyword
Balance: Frees oneself from the old, opens doors, pushes oneself and others forward.
Imbalance: Hard to listen to others, runs one's own race in a reckless manner.

The Father

The Father carries the energy of pride, strength and protection. This energy is strongly connected with the masculine energy and its qualities within us, regardless of whether we are male or female. The balanced archetype here manifests as the protective family man who cares for and protects his family. It is a person who is a warrior, strong and who manifests great results on the outside. He stands up for himself when needed and sets clear boundaries with others. The more unbalanced archetype of The Father manifests itself through some of our collective dysfunctional history. It is the father of the family who rules over the family, who judges and who has negative power. It is also the warrior in a negative sense, who uses his strength to harm himself or other people. Many of us may have been men in previous lives and participated in wars or other difficult situations, either voluntarily or by force. It may have damaged this archetype, and we may experience it as a negative to go more into our masculine energy in this life. Here we may need to work with forgiveness and through an understanding to more and more enter into our powerful and balanced masculine energy.

Keyword

Balance: Proud, strong, protective, manifests outwardly, fights for good. Imbalance: Abuser of power, protects himself too much, domineering, fights for evil, a pride that harms himself or others.

The Communicator

The Communicator carries the energy of communication and has the gift of supplying information. We mentioned this archetype briefly at the beginning of the chapter and people with this archetype's prominence are often journalists, mediums, writers, leaders, course leaders, politicians or have a position where they use a lot of communication. This archetype is positive and powerful when we are moving forward and expressing ourselves in life, even if we are to perform a life task that is about this very thing. Think of Gandhi or Martin Luther King, people who were great speakers and who through their communicative abilities reached out to large parts of the world. We may have strong communication abilities within us that, due to events in childhood or previous lives, have been dampened in various ways. Then we may have to work a lot with our expression, to use this energy in a positive way. We may have grown up in a family where we should be "seen but not heard", which has caused us to silence ourselves. The Throat Chakra often plays an important role here.

Keyword

Balance: Creates through words and expressions, speaker, leader, teacher, expresses his truth and helps himself and others.

Imbalance: Difficulty listening to others, inhibited expression, difficulty making his voice heard, uses his communicative abilities in a way that damages.

How can we work with Archetypes?

We can work with archetypes in many different ways and the important thing here is our own exploration. Archetypes are not something that is set in stone but are energetic qualities and characteristics that we have more or less of. These are energies we carry and which through awareness and healing we can strengthen and highlight more. We can have 20 different archetypes that describe our personality but maybe 5 that are more prominent and that show our great gifts.

What we want to do is look at which archetypes we recognize ourselves in or which we feel drawn to. It can show which of these are strongly present with us. We also want to look at whether we have any of these that are damaged or out of balance.

So, start by looking at the above example with archetypes. Is there anyone there that you know or think resonates strongly with you? You can also search the web to see additional examples of archetypes. But feel free to start with those included here. Maybe you feel that The Healer is a strong part within you in this life. Then look at what is written about that archetype and notice how this archetype is in its positive and balanced form.

If we then take The Healer, we see that it is a person who engages in healing of some kind, for himself or other people. This person uses their healing abilities and their interest in this in a way that uplifts and helps - but not at the expense of their own health and energy. To have balance in this archetype, boundaries, integrity and taking care of yourself are extremely important. We need to give ourselves love, replenish energy and know when we give too much to others. So, what does it look like for you here? Is there anything you can do to bring more balance to this archetype and express your gift in a powerful way? It may also be that you are drawn to healing and feel that you should work with it, while at the same time there is fear of carrying it out. Then examine this more closely. What are the fears that come up? Is it fear of what others will think or that you are not good enough? Look at what you can do to strengthen and heal these imbalances within yourself.

Do the same with other archetypes and eventually you will learn to recognize these energies more within yourself. You can also use the pendulum to ask questions. In that case, ask questions about each archetype, for example:

- Which of these archetypes do I have the strongest in this life?
- Is it The Healer archetype? The Mother? The Psychic?
- If you get one, then ask further if there is anyone else who is extra important or prominent for you in this life.

Perhaps you want to know more about why there is fear associated with a certain archetype. Then you can do the same and ask questions. If we take fear connected with healing it can look like this:

- Does this fear come from this life? (No)
- Does it come from past lives? (Yes)
- Was I a woman in that life? (Yes)
- Did I do healing/spirituality) (Yes)
- Did something happen in that life that scared me? (Yes)
- Was I killed? (No)
- Did I lose someone who meant a lot to me? (Yes)
- Pay attention to any thoughts, feelings or images that come up during this time. You can now ask more questions or ask for help to release and heal what has come up.
- *"I ask my higher self and my highest guiding team of light to release me from this fear. I choose to let go of this fear and step fully into my*

full power as a healer. Help me heal this cellular memory on all levels,
thank you!"

- Feel free to sit in this for a while and trust that you will heal.
  Then try to work on change in your practical life to reinforce
  this.

Chapter 22

A BLOCKED HEART AND THE
IMPORTANCE OF SELF LOVE

This short chapter is about love for ourselves and thus love for everything else in life. We have previously covered how you can work with the Heart Chakra, in the chapter on our chakras. In addition, we have chosen to make a separate chapter on self-love, because we believe that it is often the core of everything that happens in our lives.

Self-love is the key to all inner healing, while lack of self-love keeps us stuck in stagnation and fear. When we love ourselves deeply, we make life choices based on love, trust, creativity and expansion. When our heart is blocked, we easily end up in destructive relationships, self-criticism and negative situations. Our external relationships reflect what we feel deep down about ourselves, either consciously or unconsciously. So, you enter relationships that show you where you need to love yourself more. This can be tough to accept, but it also means that all power is in our own hands. We ourselves can create the change we want to see on the outside, by working with our interior.

Self-love is a word that comes up often, both in personal development and in spirituality. We are often told that we should love ourselves and think positive things about ourselves and of course it is important that we do that. By thinking uplifting things about ourselves, it helps to reshape and build a positive image of who we are. But loving yourself involves so much more than thinking positively about yourself. Loving oneself means feeling, seeing and knowing our true divine worth.

It's easy to love yourself when things are going well and when we get external validation. It is significantly more difficult when we lose our job, run out of money or are left by a partner. This is where the importance of self-love comes into play. We need to love ourselves no matter what we do and what happens.

Loving yourself also means that we make choices in everyday life based on self-respect. Sometimes we say we love ourselves and right after that we do something that shows the complete opposite. Here we need to examine ourselves and look at the following:

- Do I treat myself with love and respect?
- Is there a situation right now where I feel like I'm not treating myself well?
- Do I treat myself the way I would treat my very best friend?
- Do I allow myself to be exactly who I am without making excuses?
- Are there situations where I hold myself back too much?
- How and when did I get love as a child?

On our spiritual journey we will have to face ourselves and healing our heart is an important piece of the puzzle here. When we meet our Twin Flame or some other strong soul connection, we are more or less forced into our heart, sometimes quite abruptly. It is so that we will have the opportunity to heal deeply and get closer to ourselves and others. When we have big blockages in our hearts, we often have a hard time feeling love for ourselves. This means that we also have difficulty letting others in. Sometimes we have big blockages in the heart that were already created in previous lives.

If you really want to understand the relationships in your life - look at the relationship with yourself. It shows you exactly what you need to understand. Don't put anything judgmental here but see your relationships as important tools. They reflect exactly what you need to see in yourself, both positive and more challenging parts.

To summarize this part, we can say that you need to let go of limited perceptions about who you are in this life.

We often learn who we are already in childhood, mostly based on how others see us. But we need to understand that all people, including our parents have their limitations and challenges. The probability that they could see you and confirm you exactly for who you are is quite small. As an adult, you now have the opportunity to peel away all the layers that are there, all the layers that obscure and block your heart – your innermost being.

By looking at yourself with loving eyes, you see the truth about yourself. Everything you love deeply in life is a part of you. Everything you dream about is a part of you. Everything you feel true joy in is a part of you. Everything you long for is a part of you.

Behind all the heaviness and pain is the pure version of you. By freeing yourself from all the baggage that you have carried for so long, you have the opportunity to be free. Give yourself that gift in life – to find home to your heart.

Some final words

Our hope is that the text, the exercises and the energy that is with you all the time will help you on your life's journey. We also hope that the book will show you one thing – that nothing is impossible to heal. Finally, we also want to send love and gratitude to our fantastic clients we have come into contact with over the past few years. Without you, we would not have been able to make this book. By sharing your inner self and opening up to change, you are a part of this book and its contents.

In light and with great Gratitude
Martina & Hans

THANK YOU FOR YOUR TIME!

If you enjoyed this book and found it helpful, we would be so grateful if you could take a moment to share your experience by leaving a review. It can help us reach out to more people - thereby showing how we can use energy healing to heal blockages and reach our potential.

Follow our Newsletter and get your free spiritual Activation and E-Book.

Made in the USA
Monee, IL
07 April 2025

15288527R00148